EXODUS:
THE EGYPTIAN EVIDENCE

EXODUS:
THE EGYPTIAN EVIDENCE

EDITORS

Ernest S. Frerichs
Leonard H. Lesko

CONTRIBUTORS

William G. Dever
Abraham Malamat
Donald B. Redford

William A. Ward
James Weinstein
Frank J. Yurco

Winona Lake, Indiana
Eisenbrauns
1997

Library of Congress Cataloging in Publication Data

Exodus : the Egyptian Evidence / editors, Ernest S. Frerichs,
Leonard H. Lesko ; contributors, Abraham Malamat...{et al.}.

p.   cm.

Papers presented at a conference held at Brown University in 1992.

Includes bibliographical references.

ISBN 1-57506-025-6 (cloth : alk. paper)

1. Exodus, The—Congresses.   2. Bible. O.T. Exodus I–XV—Extra-
canonical parallels—Congresses.   3. Egyptian literature—Relation to
the Old Testament—Congresses.   4 Egypt—History—To 332 B.C.—
Congresses.   I. Frerichs, Ernest S.   II. Lesko, Leonard H.   III. Malamat,
Abraham.   IV. Brown University.

BS680.E9E96   1997
222'.12095—dc21   97-2703
CIP
r97

Manufactured in the United States of America
1997

In Memory of Israel Grody and Dr. Howard Paul

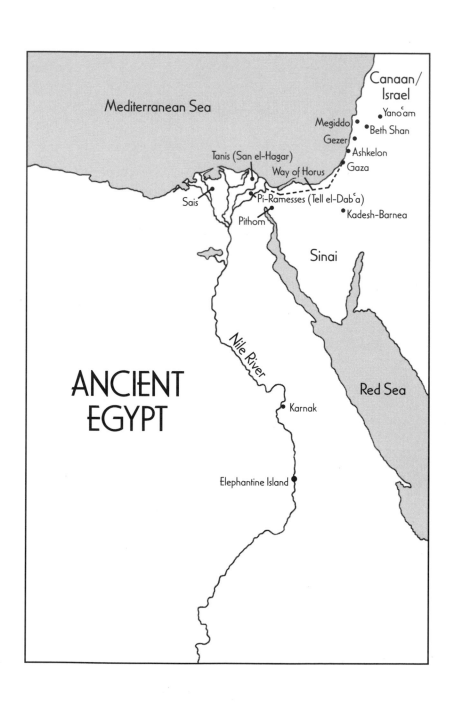

Mediterranean Sea

Canaan/
Israel

Yanoʿam

Megiddo
Beth Shan
Gezer
Ashkelon
Tanis (San el-Hagar)
Way of Horus
Gaza

Sais
Pi-Ramesses (Tell el-Dabʿa)
Pithom
Kadesh-Barnea

Sinai

Nile River

Red Sea

ANCIENT
EGYPT

Karnak

Elephantine Island

TABLE OF CONTENTS

INTRODUCTION

Ernest S. Frerichs

F ew events have impressed the memory of Jewish and Christian tradition more than the Exodus from Egypt. Generations of Americans have been moved by cinematic efforts to depict the captivating story of slaves fleeing before the mighty power of the Egyptian empire, whose rescue is effected by a water miracle. The biblical narrative of this event, embedded in the commentary and liturgy of synagogue and church, was a staple in pre-18th-century Christian and Jewish theology and history. Since the rise of humanism in the Renaissance and the development of modern literary and historical methods of criticism, however, few events have been as controversial for historians as the Exodus.

The traditional approach to the historicity of the Exodus gave large weight to the assertions of the biblical narrative, even when that narrative itself provided acknowledged ambiguities or even seeming contradictions. The focus of the traditional approach was on the history of ancient Israel; discussions of such events as the Exodus were cast in

terms that made Israelite history and Israelite origins the central concerns for evaluating evidence. The Exodus narrative provided an exciting explanation for the origin of the Israelites, their migration from slav-
ery to freedom, and the role of divine power.

Under the leadership of Brown University's Department of Egyptology, with encouragement and funding from Mr. Leonard Paul, and
with the cooperative sponsorship of Brown's Program in Judaic Studies,
Program in Ancient Studies, and Center for Old World Archaeology and
Art, a conference was convened at Brown in 1992. The attention of this
conference, however, was not on the biblical narrative, nor on ancient
Palestine, but rather on Egypt. The title of the conference indicated this
shift in focus: The Exodus: Egyptian Evidence. Professor Leonard H. Lesko,
Wilbour Professor of Egyptology and Chairman of the Department of
Egyptology, assembled a group of scholars with complementary compe-
tences from the United States, Canada, and Israel to address the conference topic. Historians, archaeologists, Egyptologists, and literary scholars
addressed this conference through the papers included in this volume.
The conference participants included specialists whose geographic concerns were primarily in ancient Egypt or in Syro-Palestine with particular
attention to early Israel. Several of the papers included have been revised
since the conference.

To balance the claims of the biblical narrative with other artifactual
and graphic evidence from Egypt and Palestine has strained the ingenu-
ity of modern scholars and resulted in the consideration of various alternatives. In the view of one of the conference participants, the challenge
to explain the Exodus and to affirm its historicity has encouraged a
rationalizing of biblical texts leading to "wishful thinking or special
pleading." The scholarly literature discussing the Exodus yields a plethora
of suggestions. There are those who understand the Exodus as a highly
complex question condensed by biblical writers with goals other than
historical accuracy, e.g., the satisfaction of the need for a dramatic story

of national origins. Indeed, such a perspective maintains that newer models of an indigenous Canaanite origin for early Israel reduce or remove any need for an exodus from Egypt. Issues of chronology have produced various dates for a single exodus and a differing thesis on whether the Exodus is a plural phenomenon in several parts across time. Exodus explanations have been linked with the volcanic eruption of Thera. The Karnak reliefs have been interpreted to yield a reading that presumes a military encounter between Egyptians and "Israelites" in a hilly area during the reign of Merenptah or Ramesses II. The historicity of Merenptah's "Israel stele" has been asserted as evidence for a military engagement, with debate on whether the Israelites involved in the encounter with Egyptians were Shasu or Canaanites, coupled with debates about the length of prior residence by the defeated Israelites. The use of Egyptian personal and place names in the biblical record has been used to argue for the probabilities of an historical exodus.

All of the above arguments and more are raised in these conference papers, though the discussions are quick to point up the limitations of any one of these explanations. Despite many differences between the perspectives of the conference participants, there is considerable agreement on the difficulties, and for some participants the impossibilities, of using Egyptian evidence to establish the historicity of the Exodus. At one extreme are those who would have questioned the need for the conference insofar as it centered its attention on Egyptian evidence for the Exodus. Another perspective, however, would be to argue not only for the need to reexamine newer evidence but to review the limits of the methodologies employed in studying the Exodus. Given that claims for ethnic identification are bound up with the question of the Exodus, it is important to discuss to what degree archaeology is capable of tracing ethnicity in material culture. The conference provided a significant opportunity for examining the limits of all methodologies as applied to the Exodus.

Those who continue to affirm the historicity of the Exodus will lean heavily on the question of a presumed positive relationship between a literary tradition of an exodus as related in the Bible and a historical memory of such an event. A bald statement of such a position would argue that the positive relationship is a reflection of reality, whatever the problems of detail may be within the textual record or between that textual record and the artifactual and graphic evidence from Egypt and Syro-Palestine.

Through the centuries both Jewish and Christian interpretations of the Exodus have lifted up characteristic readings. Midrashic traditions will emphasize the claim that the Exodus is an example of the divine redemption of Israel based on divine promises to the biblical patriarchs. A further midrashic view will see the Exodus as the basis for forming a nation of persons freed from oppression and liberated for a new life as a nation of free men. Theological readings of the Exodus dominate the history of Christian interpretation also. The emphasis on the Red Sea provided an opportunity to see water as an expression of judgment with baptism as the form of escape. A further reading of the church fathers would see the Exodus as a movement from earthly to heavenly concerns. Almost two millennia of readings, Jewish and Christian, have shown a heavy concentration on the theological dimensions of the text with some attention to philological issues.

These earlier approaches have given little consideration to the Egyptian evidence as a major determinant in establishing the historic character of the Exodus. This conference has provided a focus for that question and by so doing has increased the evidence that the argument for an historic exodus will not rest primarily, or even at all, on the Egyptian evidence. In a positive sense, the evidence of these papers should stimulate continuing discussion of the origins of early Israel based on considerations other than a single explanation of an exodus from Egypt.

1

THE EXODUS: EGYPTIAN ANALOGIES

Abraham Malamat

A t the outset, we briefly discuss the Exodus in the Bible and then consider the Egyptian material, which may serve as an analogy to the biblical account and perhaps, in part, even as an indirect proof for the Israelite episode. Before we proceed, however, it should be emphasized that none of the Egyptian sources substantiates the story of the Exodus.

The Exodus[1] figures most prominently in the biblical tradition as one of the foundations of Israelite faith, referred to in retrospect throughout the Bible more often than any other event of Israel's past—in historiography, in prophecy, and in the Psalms. Thus, the historian is faced here, first and foremost, with the dilemma of whether the story is merely the product of later contemplation, mainly of a theological nature, or indeed, an event of any historic credence. As the story is handed down to us in the form of a folktale, it is obviously not necessary to insist upon the historicity of its various elements of folklore and artifice; rather, we should focus on the substantial features, what Goethe called *die grossen Züge*, the broad sweep of affairs. I am referring to such components as the Israelites' sojourn in Egypt, the enslavement there in what the Bible terms בֵּית עֲבָדִים (*beth avadim*), "the house of bondage" (a most extraordinary coinage, which aptly characterizes totalitarian regimes throughout history); the exit and flight from Egypt into the Sinai desert; and finally, the takeover of Canaan. Do any of these components hold a kernel of historical truth, or are they merely figments of the imagination of later scribes?[2]

True, the absence of any direct extra-biblical evidence, Egyptian or otherwise, need not engender undue skepticism, which, vis-à-vis the biblical tradition, has been occasionally extreme. Rather, the indifference of external sources should merely indicate that the Exodus and the Conquest did not shake the foundations of the political and military scene of the day. These events proved central, however, to Israel's turbulent history.

As for dating the Exodus, we face the problem (known also regarding other facets of Israel's proto-history) of what I term the "telescoping process" of biblical historiography, namely, the compression of a chain of historical events into a simplified and brief account. Later editors would, in retrospect, compress a complex of events into a severely curtailed timespan.[3] We face the alternatives of a relatively brief streamlined exodus, as told in the Bible—a "punctual" event—or a "durative" event, postulating two or more exoduses, or even a steady flow of Israelites coming out of Egypt during a lengthy period, perhaps encompassing hundreds of years. In the latter case, the search for a specific date of the Exodus is a futile undertaking, as a time span ranging from the 15th to 12th centuries B.C.E. may be involved. Yet even so, we may assume a peak period for a stream of Israelites coming out of Egypt—let us call it the Moses movement—whereby we are confronted with the delineation of a definite chronology for the Exodus. Here we have to take into account Egyptian history as well as the history of the "West," (i.e., Anatolia, Syria, and Palestine).

Like many scholars, I used to accept the reign of Ramesses II, more precisely the period subsequent to the famous Battle of Kadesh between Ramesses II and the Hittites in the former's fifth year (now dated around 1273 B.C.E.), as the opportune time for the Exodus. The battle seemed to have been—in contrast to their Egyptian sources—a fiasco for the Egyptians, who were then undergoing a process of temporary decline, especially in Canaan, where the local rulers revolted. Such a situation in the wake of the Battle of Kadesh could well have facilitated, in a broad manner of speaking, an Israelite exodus.

Now, however, I tend to lower the date of a "punctual" exodus—the climactic stage within a durative event—toward the end of the XIXth Dynasty (the late 13th century B.C.E. and the early years of the 12th century). This period saw the breakdown of both the Egyptian and Hittite empires—in modern terminology, the collapse of the bipolar political system of the day. The simultaneous decline of the two provided a rare opportunity for the oppressed, the small peoples and ethnic minorities from Anatolia to lower Egypt—in Machiavellian terms, the "occasione." It is in this fluid context that we may find the true setting that enabled the Israelites to set out from Egypt for Canaan.

While there is no direct extra-biblical source on the Exodus (or Conquest) or on the Israelite servitude in Egypt, we do posses several significant *indirect* sources—a sort of circumstantial evidence that lends greater authority to the biblical account. I shall just mention some of the more illuminating of these sources, well known in research, and shall at the end dwell upon two such items. The first is often referred to in the debate on the Exodus but perhaps not analyzed comprehensively. The second, a recent discovery, has been hardly dealt with concerning our issue.

(1) A well-known biblical passage, usually drawn into the discussion

of the Exodus (Exodus 1:11), is the building of the store-cities Pithom and Ramesses by the enslaved Israelites. Despite the alleged relevancy of this passage, many scholars see here an anachronistic statement of much later times[4] and find other difficulties, such as the form of the biblical toponym "Ramesses" instead of the standard Egyptian name of "Pi-Ramesses."

(2) Connected in some way with this passage and serving as probable evidence of the Israelite servitude in Egypt is Papyrus Leiden 348. It is a decree by an official of Ramesses II concerning construction work at his new capital of Pi-Ramesses, declaring, "Distribute grain rations to the soldiers and to the ʿApiru who transport stones to the great pylon of Ramesses."

(2a) More recently, a similar document was published,[5] an undated ostracon in hieratic script, again referring to the ʿApiru, engaged in construction work at the city of Pi-Ramesses. We can not enter here into the ʿApiru problem and its complex relation with the Habiru and Hebrew. Suffice it to state that we concur with many scholars in assuming that the Hebrews are somehow connected linguistically and ethnically with the ʿApiru. This assumption may rule out the connection often surmised of the Hebrews/Israelites with the Shasu.[6] If so, the Hebrews were engaged in forced labor at the construction of the capital city of Ramesses. The problem, which remains outside the scope of the Egyptian context, is the affiliation between the Israelites and the Hebrews, the latter designating a broader ethnicity. In short, each and every Israelite is a Hebrew and likely an ʿApiru, while not every Hebrew or ʿApiru is necessarily an Israelite. Thus, even here there is no definite proof that Israelites were engaged in the city's building. At best, we have in this case merely circumstantial evidence of a questionable nature. But this remains the utter limit for the historian of the Exodus; he can go no further. Evidence of a more "scientific" caliber is no longer within the reach of historical research.

(3) Everyone here has dealt with the Merneptah Stele of the fifth

year of this pharaoh, now to be dated to 1208 B.C.E.[7] The only statement I wish to make in this context is that this stele has little or nothing to do with the Exodus. It merely attests to the actual presence of a group designated "Israel" in Canaan towards the end of the 13th century B.C.E. What tribes this Israelite group included is unknown, yet in view of the geographical sequence in the text, Israel could presumably be found in northern Palestine or in its hinterland.

(4) The next possible connection between the biblical tradition and the Egyptian sources is of quite a different nature. Exodus 13:17 states, "When Pharaoh let the people go, God did not lead them by way of the land of the Philistines, although that was near; for God said: 'Lest the people repent when they see war and return to Egypt.'" This passage about the journey of the Israelites through Sinai may be better understood if we take into account the military road that the Egyptians constructed along the coast of northern Sinai, the biblical "way of the Philistines." This route was fortified with a tight network of strongholds by Seti I early in the 13th century B.C.E. and remained under strict control of the Egyptians throughout that century.[8] It might easily have become a trap for the wandering Israelites; hence the command attributed to God. The Bible continues, quoting Pharaoh in Exodus 14:3; "For Pharaoh will say of the people of Israel 'They are entangled in the land [i.e., Sinai]; the wilderness has shut them in,'" reflecting the Egyptian view that because of the fortification line the Israelites were forced to make a detour and venture into the desert.

(5) Particularly significant typologically are the following documents reporting on Egyptian frontier officials stationed on the border zone between Egypt and Sinai (located along the northern section of the present-day Suez Canal). The texts are contained in several of the Papyri Anastasi (purchased as early as 1839) which were originally used as schoolboys' copy books of model letters. Some of them reveal the tight control of the Egyptian authorities over their eastern frontier in the last

decades of the 13th century. Each and every group or individual, whether Egyptian or foreign, could neither enter nor leave Egypt without a special permit. I view this situation as an "Iron Curtain," an idiom coined by Winston Churchill in his famous speech in 1946 at Westminster College in Fulton, Missouri. The Iron Curtain functioned in both directions of the passage—entrance and exit. Indeed, without this fortification line entire minority groups, and probably Egyptians as well would have escaped from the delta into Sinai and Palestine. This also sheds light on the persistent pleas to Pharaoh by Moses and Aaron, "Let my people go!"

(5a) Thus Papyrus Anastasi III[9] records daily crossings of individuals in either direction in the time of Merneptah.

(5b) Anastasi VI[10] illustrates the passage into Egypt of an entire tribe coming down from Edom during a drought. This report is reminiscent of several patriarchal episodes concerning Abraham and Jacob, who were also said to have descended into Egypt because of a drought.

(6) But most exciting for our purpose is Papyrus Anastasi V,[11] dating to the end of the XIXth Dynasty (the end of the 13th century), which reports the escape of two slaves or servants from the royal residence at Pi-Ramesses, on the western edge of Wadi Tumilat. The fugitives flee into the Sinai wilderness by way of the fortified border. The writer of the letter, a high-ranking Egyptian military commander, had been ordered by the Egyptian authorities to ensure that the runaways were captured and returned to Egypt:

> Another matter, to wit: I was sent forth from the broad-halls of the palace—life, prosperity, health!—in the third month of the third season, day 9, at the time of evening, following after these two slaves. Now when I reached the enclosure-wall of Tjeku on the 3rd month of the third season, day 10, they told [me] they were saying to the south that they had passed by on the 3rd month of the third season, day 10. (xx 1) [Now] when [I] reached the fortress, they told me that the *scout* had come from the desert [saying that] they had passed the walled place

north of the Migdol of Seti Mer-ne-Ptah—life, prosperity health!—Beloved like Seth.

When my letter reaches you, write to me about all that has happened to [them]. Who found their tracks? Which watch found their tracks? What people are after them? Write to me about all that has happened to them and how many people you send out after them.

[May your health] be good!

Anastasi V[12]

We witness here several striking parallels to the Exodus episode—in miniature of course—as opposed to the biblical 600,000 foot soldiers setting out from Egypt (Exodus 12:37). (A note on the figure 600,000:[13] There is no doubt that we have here a typological number. As I have shown elsewhere, the Bible refers quite often to 600 soldiers, or multiples thereof, conveying, to my mind, the idea of the size of a platoon or regiment. The 600,000 are likely comprised of 1,000 platoons, while the number 1,000 is again to be taken as typological [see Deuteronomy 1:11], implying a multitude of soldiers, an expression actually used in the Exodus story [Exodus 1: 9, 20].)

We can outline four parallel features between Anastasi V and the Exodus episode:

1) The escape of slaves, or semi-slaves, from the area of the city of Ramesses in search of freedom.

2) Egyptian military forces pursue the runaways in order to return them to Egypt.

3) The escape route into Sinai is roughly identical with the biblical report: After leaving Ramesses we find the two Egyptians in Tjeku, most likely biblical Sukkoth (with all due reservation), the second station on the Exodus route (still in Wadi Tumilat). We then hear of the escapees near Migdol (the text has *sgwr* = a fortress in the Canaanite language, like *migdol*) or perhaps north of it. Migdol, well known in the Bible and

mentioned as another station in the Exodus route, is beyond the present Suez Canal, north of el-Kantara. In 1920 Alan Gardiner identified the city with Tell el-Her, which was excavated by Eliezer Oren in the 1970s.[14] Significantly, the fleeing Israelites turned north of Migdol and camped between the city and the Mediterranean (Exodus 14:2).

4) The flight took place under the cover of darkness, as one would expect, and as is hinted by the pursuing Egyptian official, who left a short time after the escapees from the capital city, "at the time of evening, following after these two slaves." Similarly, we may remember that the Israelite Exodus started בַּחֲצֹת הַלַּיְלָה, "at midnight" (Exodus 11:4).

THE ELEPHANTINE STELE

Finally, we come to a document from Elephantine,[15] published recently by D. Bidoli, which is a royal stele from the second (?) year of Pharaoh Sethnakht, founder of the XXth Dynasty. The stele, dating in absolute chronology from the first or second decade of the 12th century B.C.E., has been newly edited by Rosemarie Drenkhahn in her monograph *Die Elephantine-Stele des Sethnacht* (1980) and more recently was dealt with by Friedrich Junge. It reflects the final years of the XIXth Dynasty and the first two years of Sethnakht. For our purpose, it is important to mention that the political situation in Egypt at that time was marred by the enigmatic intervention of Asiatics (*sṯtw*), who were approached and bribed by a faction of Egyptians, let us call it A, who revolted against another faction, let us call it B, who remained loyal to Sethnakht. The Egyptians bribed the Asiatics with silver and gold, as well as copper, "the possession of Egypt," in order that they assist faction A in their plot. However, Sethnakht foiled faction A and drove the Asiatics out of Egypt, forcing them to embark upon an exodus of sorts, which led them towards southern Palestine.

As for the delivery of the precious metals to the Asiatics (which were eventually recovered by faction B), three Exodus passages may be of unexpected significance:[16] Exodus 3:21-22, 11:2, and 12:35-36. They read, according to the Revised Standard Version:

> "And when you go you shall not go empty, but each woman shall take of her neighbor, and of her who sojourn in her house, objects of silver and gold, and clothing ... thus you shall despoil the Egyptians" (Exodus 3:21-22); "... that they (the people) ask every man of his neighbor (and every woman of her neighbor), objects of silver and of gold" (Exodus 11:2); "The people of Israel had also done as Moses told them, for they had asked of the Egyptians objects of silver and of gold, and clothing. And the Lord had given the people favor in the sight of the Egyptians, so that they let them have what they asked. Thus they despoiled the Egyptians."
>
> Exodus 12:35-6; see also Psalm 105:37

We have here an interesting analog between the Egyptian stele and an awkward tradition within the Exodus story (which, admittedly, does not belong to the *"grossen Züge"*), according to which the Israelites, prior to their impending exodus, receive or appropriate precious objects from the Egyptians (in all three cases here, שאל means to "appropriate," rather than the usual meaning, "to ask" or "to borrow"). This would liken the Israelites to the Asiatics of the Elephantine Stele, both of whom were given the same objects by the Egyptians. Of course, we may simply have here parallel literary motifs. But note also the biblical statement, put into Pharaoh's mouth, which is often overlooked: "Come let us deal shrewdly with them (i.e., the Israelites) ... and if war befall us, they join our enemies and fight against us and escape from the land" (Exodus 1:10). Here we can witness the trauma that befell the Egyptians because of the Israelites (Elephantine Stele: Asiatics), who could become a potential threat if they chose to join the enemies of Egypt.

In sum, although an Israelite exodus is not mentioned in Egyptian sources, a number of important analogs are apparent, beginning perhaps with the time of the Hyksos. These analogs become more concentrated around 1200 B.C.E. and are suggestive of the biblical event.[17]

EXCURSUS: IRSU AND BEYA

T he sequence and chronology of the last rulers of the XIXth Dynasty is now believed to be as follows: Seti II (1203-1197 B.C.E.), during whose reign several of the Papyri Anastasi were composed, was followed by his son Siptah (1197-1192 B.C.E.), after whose death Queen Tausert (1192-1190 B.C.E.), the widow of Seti II and regent during the reign of Siptah, ascended the throne. Then, in the aftermath of bitter internal struggles, the future Pharaoh Sethnakht (1190-1188 B.C.E.) became the founder of the XXth Dynasty.[18]

It is within this period, especially during the later part, that we should place the Syrian-Palestinian usurpation of Egypt as described in Papyrus Harris 1, which portrays the desolate conditions prior to the reign of Ramesses III. The leader of the Asiatic intruders was someone called Irsu. For our purpose, it does not matter whether we have here a personal name or an Egyptian phrase meaning "he made himself," as held by many Egyptologists. At any rate, the papyrus contains the determinative '3mw, designating a Semitic Syrian or a Semitic Palestinian. On the assumption that we have here a personal name, various identifications have been suggested.[19] Some connection with the Asiatics of the Elephantine Stele is not altogether implausible and certainly seems intriguing.

The common contemporary, albeit doubtful, belief identifies Irsu with Beya, a prominent Egyptian official who was active from the reign of Seti II until Tausert, bearing a possibly Semitic name and known in modern parlance as the "king maker." Should this identification prove true, then a recently discovered letter (in Akkadian) sent by Beya to the last ruler of Ugarit may enable us to date the Semitic usurpation of

Egypt more precisely, i.e., about 1195-1190 B.C.E.[20] Furthermore, there are now a few scholars who boldly maintain that Beya/Irsu is in fact the biblical Moses,[21] bringing us back to the very subject of our paper. But such an assumption is hardly supported by any documentation, and so it remains highly speculative.

ENDNOTES

[1] From the plethora of studies on the biblical Exodus in the Egyptian context, we may cite a few of recent date: H. Cazelles, *Autour de l'Exode* (Paris, 1987), esp. pp. 189-231, and "Peut-on circonscrire un evenement Exode?" in *La protohistoire d'Israel*, ed. E.-M. Laperrousaz (Paris, 1990), pp. 29-65; N.M. Sarna, *Exploring Exodus* (New York, 1986); W.H. Stiebing, *Out of the Desert?* (Buffalo, NY, 1989); M. Görg, "Exodus," in *Neues Bibel-Lexikon*, ed. Görg and B. Lang, Lieferung 4 (1990), cols. 631-636; K.A. Kitchen, "Exodus, The," in *Anchor Bible Dictionary*, ed. D.N. Freedman (New York, 1992), vol. 2, pp. 700-708.

[2] A. Malamat, "The Proto-History of Israel: A Study in Method," in *The Word of the Lord Shall Go Forth: Essays in Honor of David Noel Freedman*, ed. Carol Meyers and M. O'Connor (Philadelphia, 1983), pp. 303-313.

[3] Malamat, "Proto-History," pp. 307f.

[4] See esp. D.B. Redford, "Exodus 1:11," *Vetus Testamentum* 13 (1963), pp. 401-418, and "An Egyptological Perspective on the Exodus Narrative," in *Egypt, Israel, Sinai*, ed. A.F. Rainey (Tel Aviv, 1987), pp. 137-161. This author assumes a sixth-century B.C.E. (or even later) date; cf. also B.J. Diebner, "Erwägungen zum Thema 'Exodus,'" *Studien zur Altägyptischen Kultur* 11 (1984), pp. 596-630. In contrast, Stiebing (*Out of the Desert?*) refutes such a late date and on the other hand rejects the extreme early-15th-century B.C.E. date.

[5] See Cazelles, "The Hebrews," in *Peoples of the Old Testament*, ed. D.J. Wiseman (Oxford, 1973), p. 14.

[6] An identity propagated esp. by R. Giveon in his book *Les bédouins Shosou des documents égyptiens* (Leiden, 1971).

[7] The most recent studies of this document from a historical viewpoint are H. Engel, "Die Siegesstele des Merneptah," *Biblica* 60 (1979), pp. 373-399; L.E. Stager, "Merenptah, Israel and the Sea Peoples," *Eretz-Israel* 18 (1985), 56*-64*; F.J. Yurco, "Merenptah's Canaanite Campaign," *Journal of the American Research Center in Egypt* 23 (1986); J.J. Bimson, "Merenptah's Israel and Recent Theories of Israelite Origins," *Journal for the Study of the Old Testament* 49 (1991), pp. 3-29.

[8] A. Gardiner, "The Ancient Military Road Between Egypt and Palestine," *Journal of Egyptian Archaeology* 6 (1920), pp. 99-116; E.D. Oren, "'Ways of Horus' in North Sinai," in Rainey, *Egypt, Israel, Sinai*, pp. 69-119.

[9] J.B. Pritchard, ed., *Ancient Near Eastern Texts Relating to the Old Testament*, 3d ed. (Princeton, 1969), pp. 258f.; R.M. Caminos, *Late-Egyptian Miscellanies* (Oxford, 1954), pp. 69ff.

[10] Pritchard, *Texts*, p. 259; Caminos, *Late-Egyptian Miscellanies*, pp. 293-296; and H. Goedicke, "Papyrus Anastasi VI 51-61," *Studien zur Altägyptischen Kultur* 14 (1987), pp. 83-98.

[11] "The Pursuit of Runaway Slaves," in Pritchard, *Texts*, p. 259; see Caminos, *Late-Egyptian Miscellanies*, pp. 254-258.

[12] Pritchard, *Texts*, p. 259.

[13] See Malamat, "The Danite Migration and the Pan-Israelite Exodus-Conquest," *Biblica* 51 (1970), pp. 9f.

[14] For Gardiner, see "Military Road," pp. 107-109; see also Oren, "Migdol: A New Fortress on the Edge of the Eastern Nile Delta," *Bulletin of the American Schools of Oriental Research* 256 (1984), pp. 7-44.

[15] Published by D. Bidoli in *Mitteilungen des deutschen archäologischen Instituts, Kairo* 28 (1972), pp. 195-200, pl. 49; and investigated by R. Drenkhahn, *Die Elephantine-Stele des Sethnacht* (Wiesbaden, 1980); cf. A. Spalinger, review of *Elephantine-Stele*, by Drenkhahn, *Bibliotheca Orientalis* 39 (1982), cols. 272-288. For a revised reading see F. Junge in *Elephantine* 11 (1988), pp. 55-58.

[16] Some vague allusions to a biblical-Egyptian connection have already been made; cf. Görg, *Kairos* 20 (1978), pp. 279f. and n. 28; J.C. de Moor, *The Rise of Yahwism* (Leuven, 1990), pp. 136ff.; M. Dijkstra, *Nederlands Theologisch Tijdschrift* 45 (1991), pp. 1-15.

[17] For such a dating, based on different reasons, see M.B. Rowton, "The Problem of the Exodus," *Palestine Exploration Quarterly* 85 (1953), pp. 46-60; cf. Görg, "Exodus," col. 635; de Moor, *Rise of Yahwism*, p. 150. See also G.A. Rendsburg, "The Date of the Exodus," *Vetus Testamentum* 42 (1992), pp. 510-527.

[18] Gardiner, *Egypt of the Pharaohs* (Oxford, 1966), pp. 277-280; L.H. Lesko, "A Little More Evidence for the End of the 19th Dynasty," *Journal of the American Research Center in Egypt* 5 (1966), pp. 29-32; Drenkhahn, *Elephantine-Stele*.

[19] See my own attempt made more than forty years ago, "Cushan Rishataim and the Decline of the Near East Around 1200 B.C.E.," *Journal of Near Eastern Studies* 13 (1954), pp. 231ff.; see also, from among many studies, J.-M. Kruchten, "La fin de la XIXe Dynastie vue d'après la section 'historique' du Papyrus Harris I," *Annuaire de l'Institut de philologie et d'historie orientales et slaves* 25 (1981), pp. 51-64.

[20] On (Irsu-) Beya, see most recently (and there the earlier literature) M. Yon, *In the Crisis Years: The 12th Century B.C.E.*, ed. W.A. Ward and M. Sharp Joukowsky (Dubuque, IA, 1992), pp. 119f.; C. Maderna-Sieben, "Der historische Abschnitt des Papyrus Harris I," *Göttinger Miszellen* 123 (1991), pp. 57-90, esp. 87 (the equation of Irsu-Beya, suggested first, hesitantly, by J. Černý and Gardiner, became here already "sicherlich").

[21] See E.A. Knauf, *Midian* (Wiesbaden, 1988), pp. 135ff.; de Moor, *Rise of Yahwism*, chap. 4.6: Beya-Moses, pp. 136-151.

ADDENDUM:

This paper was written for the colloquy "The Exodus" at Brown University in the spring of 1992. The publication of the proceedings was much delayed; in the meantime the paper of J. de Moor, "Egypt, Ugarit and Exodus," in *Ugarit, Religion and Culture*, ed. N. Wyatt et al. (Munster, 1996), pp. 213-247, appeared. The author independently uses much of the material dealt with above and concludes, as we do, that the Exodus, or its dominant phase, took place around 1190 B.C.E. However, he still maintains, I believe unjustifiably, his previous identification of Moses and other biblical figures—A.M.

2

MERENPTAH'S CANAANITE CAMPAIGN AND ISRAEL'S ORIGINS

Frank J. Yurco

n his article "Merenptah's Israel and Recent Theories of Israelite Origins"[1] John J. Bimson reviewed the recent scholarship on the beginnings of Israel, with special focus on Merenptah's Canaanite campaign and the earliest attested reference to Israel in a text, which was contained in Merenptah's Year 5 Victory Stela, Cairo (No. 34025, verso). The reference comes in a retrospective section of the stela, after its main subject, the defeat of the Libyans and Sea Peoples, and in a sense is a summation of Merenptah's accomplishments in maintaining the Egyptian empire intact. Bimson correctly notes that this stela was relatively neglected, following the initial excitement generated by its discovery by Flinders Petrie, in 1896, in the ruins of Merenptah's funerary temple, in western Thebes. Indeed, the reason for this is that many scholars dismissed it as typical pharaonic hyperbole and exaggeration because of the highly poetic nature of the text and the absence of confirming documentation. It was Kenneth Kitchen who began the reassessment of

Merenptah's texts while preparing his magnificent corpus of Ramesside inscriptions. He pointed out that Merenptah's epithet, "Binder of Gezer," as found in the pharaoh's titulary, echoed claims made on the stela, which has become known as the "Israel" Stela.

What renewed the discussion and reassessment of the stela and its text was my discovery of Merenptah's Canaanite campaign battle reliefs carved on the western outer wall of the court at the Karnak temple, known as the Cour de la Cachette, situated just south of the great Hypostyle Hall of Sety I and Ramesses II.[2] Conventionally, Egyptologists have agreed that such battle reliefs are prime evidence of the historicity of military campaigns. Most Egyptologists, and significantly Kenneth Kitchen, accepted my findings. The few who disagreed included Donald B. Redford, who denied any real Canaanite campaign by Merenptah, and reassigned the Karnak reliefs back to Ramesses II.[3] His argument was based largely on the names of the pharaoh's chariot teams, which he claimed were strictly those of Ramesses II. Yet, a check of chariot teams' names throughout the XIXth and early XXth Dynasty shows that Sety I, Ramesses II, Merenptah, and Ramesses III all used the very same names for their royal chariot teams.[4] Further, Redford had dismissed summarily the evidence of the usurped cartouches found in Merenptah's battle reliefs, claiming that they were beyond analysis—a view that even a cursory glance at the reliefs and their cartouches would dispute and that I disproved in my epigraphic study (seconded by Kitchen). Beyond any doubt, these cartouches were originally carved under Merenptah, so the battle reliefs are his.[5]

These battle reliefs of Merenptah depict four battle scenes, with three against fortified city-states (Ashkelon is specifically named in one, while the other two, though not named in the reliefs, may be surmised to be Gezer and Yano'am from the "Israel" Stela). The fourth battle scene, though badly damaged by the loss of its upper portion, does retain clear evidence of battle in hilly country, against a foe depicted as Canaanites that had no fortified city. These four battle scenes of Merenptah and their data correspond exactly to the retrospective text on Merenptah's "Israel" Stela, where Ashkelon, Gezer, Yanoʿam, and Israel are all named specifically; and most significantly, the determinative used for the writing of the name Israel in the stela suits exactly the fourth battle scene, depicting a people in open country without a fortified town.[6] This combination, three battle scenes against city-states, one named Ashkelon, and a battle in open, hilly country, matches precisely the Merenptah "Israel" Stela's retrospective account, and it is a reasonable analysis that the stela and the Karnak battle reliefs record one and the same military campaign. These four are the only battle scenes in the Merenptah reliefs at Karnak. They match exactly this same pharaoh's Canaanite campaign mentioned retrospectively in the stela, and no other war in Canaan by this pharaoh is attested in any of his monuments. Thus it is pointless to argue that scene four of the reliefs, by my analysis, is anything other than Israel—a position taken by Rainey[7] and also suggested by Bimson.[8] What troubles some scholars is that scene four (Israel) includes a chariot that by its disposition must belong to the foe. Secondly, Merenptah's foes in this scene are dressed in the same style as the Canaanites of the other three city-states attacked by Merenptah and shown in his reliefs.

Among the questions raised is how the Israelites in this early era could have obtained chariots. In Bimson's reasoning, the Israelites were already well established in the hill country of Canaan. The long, quiet, peaceful conclusion to Ramesses II's reign (1279-1212 B.C.E.), especially after the peace treaty with Hatti of year 21, he reasoned, offered the Israelites the possibility to settle in the highlands of Canaan.

Papyrus Anastasi I, a literary controversy between two scribes about Syro-Palestinian geography, is generally agreed upon as describing Canaan and Syria under Ramesses II.[9] It describes the hill country as wooded, wild, sparsely settled, and haunted by Semitic-speaking Shasu nomads. Only loosely controlled by the Egyptians and their Canaanite vassals, this hill country was ideal for malcontents from the cities, for pastoralists, for the Shasu nomads, or for other dispossesed peoples to settle without arousing Egyptian or Canaanite suspicions. Yet the papyrus also indicates that such settlement in large numbers didn't happen prior to the latter part of Ramesses II's reign. Egypt's main concern and control was exercised over the coastal plain, with its cities and towns and their hinterlands. Additionally, Egypt tightly controlled Beth Shan and the Megiddo area in northern Canaan, a strategic area where routes to the Transjordan area and to Egypt's northern province, Kharu, met and crossed.[10] Accordingly, the central hill country of Canaan, south of Beth Shan and Megiddo and north of Jerusalem—another Egyptian-controlled anchor point—was the logical area for initial Israelite penetration and settlement, indeed, an area where Lawrence Stager has found early evidence of Israelite settlement.[11] This accords with Israel appearing in Merenptah's campaign as a new, previously unattested people, and it explains how they could have been Pharaoh's major foe. It is likely that their meddling with the towns of Ashkelon, Gezer, and Yanoʿam prompted Merenptah's campaign. The advent of a new pharaoh traditionally was a time for unrest among Egypt's vassals. This analysis also suggests how these early Israelites came to possess chariots; they got them from the city-states by connivance or capture, for there were chariots in these cities. Or, as Papyrus Anastasi I suggests, the occasional Egyptian passing through the hill country might be ambushed and his chariot stolen.

Following his campaign, Merenptah extended Egyptian military control into the highlands of Canaan.[12] He also reasserted Egyptian hegemony over the coastal cities and towns. These measures carried Egyptian dominion of Canaan and Kharu safely through the later, troubled XIXth Dynasty reigns. Artifacts bearing the names of Sety II, Siptah, and Tawosret have been found at numerous locales in Canaan.[13] Ramesses III, early in his reign, further consolidated Egyptian dominion by establishing governors and building residences for them throughout Canaan, as Eliezer Oren has demonstrated; and taxes were assessed also, as Orly Goldwasser has shown.[14] Accordingly, early Israelite efforts to expand were crippled severely by the joint efforts of Merenptah and Ramesses III. So thoroughly were the Israelites subdued that it wasn't until the time of the Judge Deborah that a few tribes could be mustered to mount an attack on the Canaanites in Megiddo.[15] Egypt's firm control of Canaan was sorely shaken by the onslaught of the Sea Peoples when they came by land and sea in the eighth year of Ramesses III's reign. This was the first major thrust of Sea Peoples into Canaan, although certain Sea Peoples are attested earlier.[16] Ramesses III claimed that he settled defeated Peleset (Philistines) and Tjekker and established them in strongholds under his name.[17] Effectively, this meant that the Sea Peoples, after their repulse from Egypt proper, were allowed by the Egyptians to settle in coastal Canaan. Egypt did continue to control, barely, the inland parts of Canaan, as indicated by the find of a statue base of Ramesses VI in Megiddo and other monuments of this pharaoh, including statues in a warlike pose.[18] By the time of Wen-Amun (late Dynasty XX-early Dynasty XXI), the Philistines and the Tjekker firmly ruled coastal Canaan, and Egyptian hegemony was long gone. Finally, as the Song of Deborah shows, the Israelites were able to move against the Canaanites in the lowlands, but the fact that Ramesses III had allowed the Philistines and the Tjekker to seize possession of the coastal areas blocked Israel's ambition to expand there also; the Philistine superiority in culture, political organization, and technology, including a monopoly over iron working, further hindered the Israelites.[19] This is reflected clearly by the many difficulties experienced by Israel in the Book of Judges.

The other main disagreement between Bimson's position and mine concerns the versification of the closing lines of Merenptah's "Israel" Stela. My position is that the versification reflects Egypt's political control and administration of its Syro-Palestinian realm, which was divided into the provinces of Canaan and Kharu. That doesn't translate into prior assumptions, as Bimson claimed.[20] The political and administrative structures of Canaan and Kharu are not reflections of the poetry in the Merenptah Stela; rather, it is the poetry of the stela that reflects the reality of the Egyptian administrative divisions of Canaan and Kharu, along with the greater political world of the Late Bronze Age. At the conclusion of the regnal year 5 victory over the Libyans and their Sea Peoples allies, Merenptah could fairly claim that he had maintained the realm handed to him by Ramesses II. As the "Israel" Stela states, Libya was devastated, while Hatti kept the peace. That the Hittites had remained at peace is indicated by Merenptah's statement in his great victory inscription at Karnak (found on the inner eastern wall of the Cour de la Cachette) that he had been sending grain to the Hittites and, further, by a sword found in Ugarit stamped with Merenptah's cartouche.[21] These references indicate economic and military assistance to the Hittite realm, as stipulated in the terms of the peace treaty drawn by Ramesses II and Hattusilis III in Ramesses II's 21st regnal year (1258 B.C.E.).

TEXT CONTINUES ON PAGE 38

Semites in Egypt *(see chapter 4). Bearing the title Hyksos, a figure named Abisha (leaning over an ibex at center, opposite, top) leads his Semitic clansmen into Egypt to conduct trade. This scene dates to about 1890 B.C.E. and is preserved at Beni Hasan, halfway between Cairo and Luxor. The Hyksos were Canaanites who ruled Egypt for roughly two and a half centuries, starting about 1800 B.C.E. "Hyksos" is a Greek term meaning "ruler of foreign lands" or "shepherd kings." Foreign groups often sojourned in Egypt, especially in the pursuit of commerce.*

Recalling the Israelites of the Bible, a wall painting (opposite, bottom) depicts workmen laboring at the task of brick making. What we know from historical records supports details regarding this task in the biblical account. One Egyptian text bemoans the lack of straw for brick making. This detail is also noted in the Bible; that straw was used at all reveals a familiarity with Egyptian life, since straw was not used typically in Canaan for making mudbricks. More generally, the biblical account of the oppressive increase in forced labor may reflect the building boom in the eastern delta under Ramesses II. Photos by Erich Lessing.

Victims of Progress. *These large storage vessels, called collar-rim jars, are character-istic of early Israelite culture, although not exclusively so (see chapter 4). Notable for the collar-like ridge at the top of their short, wide necks, the jars could hold about 10 to 15 gallons of water. Some scholars believe the were the primary means of moving and storing water in the Canaanite hill country until about 1000 B.C.E.* Photo by David Harris/Israel Museum.

The Merenptah Stele. *Discovered a century ago at Thebes, this 7.5-foot-high black granite slab was commissioned by Merenptah during his fifth regnal year (1207 B.C.E.) to boast of his military successes. He proclaims, "Canaan has been plundered into every sort of woe; Ashkelon has been overcome; Gezer has been captured. Yano'am was made nonexistent; Israel is laid waste, his seed is not." Unpronounced signs, called determinatives, indicate that while the first three names are cities, the fourth is the name of a people, not a place. Merenptah thus provides the earliest nonbiblical reference to Israel.* Photo by Jürgen Liepe.

↑ ↗
Ashkelon Besieged *(above and opposite). According to author Frank Yurco, Merenptah put his military victories into pictorial form on the outer western wall of the Cour de la Cachette, at the Karnak temple. Four of the scenes correspond to his boasts on the Merenptah Stele. The first shows Ashkelon under attack, as inhabitants gather atop a crenelated tower and seem to beseech the heavens for aid.* Photo by Garo Nalbandian. Drawing from W. Wreszinski, *Atlas zur Altägyptischen kultur-geschichte.*

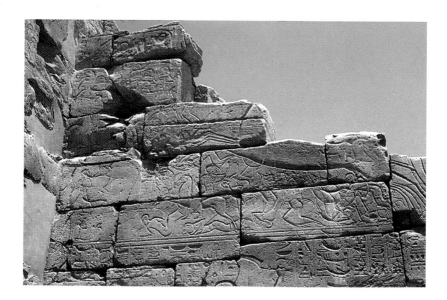

"Yano'am Was Made Nonexistent" *declares the Merenptah Stele; the corresponding depiction from the Karnak temple appears at opposite, bottom (and drawing below). Some of the city's defenders appear along the crenelated walls at upper left, while others tumble helplessly before the oversize Egyptian chariot team.* Photo by Garo Nalbandian. Drawing from W. Wreszinski, *Atlas zur Altägyptischen kultur-geschichte.*

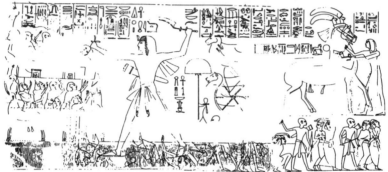

Gezer Succumbs. *The defenders of Gezer cower helplessly before the mighty pharaoh (top, drawing above). Note that the three cities mentioned in the Merenptah Stele and portrayed at Karnak—Ashkelon, Yanoʿam, and Gezer—are all depicted similarly: the besieged cities at left, balanced by Pharaoh and his forces at right.*
Drawing from W. Wreszinski, *Atlas zur Altägyptischen kulturgeschichte.*

Next, Merenptah's Stela mentions the plundering of Canaan, followed by two pairs of couplets describing the four battles fought by Merenptah against Ashkelon, Gezer, Yanoʿam, and the people of Israel. As the battle reliefs and texts demonstrate, this military activity all happened within the province of Canaan. Moreover, the stela's text adds that Kharu, Egypt's other Syro-Palestinian province, had become a widow because of Egypt. Quite naturally, this line forms a framing couplet with the line mentioning the plundering of Canaan. Geographically, this versification reflects the provincial level of the Egyptian realm. In the closing lines, Merenptah adds that all restless peoples are now stilled. This, together with the reference to Libya being devastated and Hatti remaining at peace, forms the outer framing couplet. Geographically, this outer couplet reflects the highest level of administration, that is, Egypt's relation with outside powers. So, the versification proposed in my article echoes faithfully Egypt's geopolitical world. It echoes the fact that Merenptah had successfully preserved Ramesses II's realm. Yet it does not preclude the view that Israel could have been Merenptah's principal foe in the Canaanite campaign.[22]

Bimson's problem with the stela's versification was his inadequate consideration of the Egyptian administration, and political structure, of

Are These the Israelites? *Author Frank Yurco believes that this panel (below, drawing at bottom) from the Karnak temple illustrates the reference to the Israelites in the Merenptah Stele. Note that this scene depicts not the defense of a city but a battle in an open field, lending weight to the idea that "Israel" was the name of a people and not a place. Significantly, those vanquished here are shown wearing ankle-length skirts identical to the skirts shown in scenes that unquestionably portray Canaanites. If Yurco is right, this relief bolsters the view that the Israelites emerged out of Canaanite society.* Photo from Frank Yurco, *Journal of the American Research Center in Egypt 23 (1986).* Drawing by Paul Hoffman/F. Schonbach.

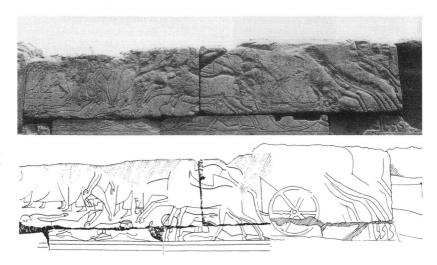

"No, *These* Are the Israelites," *counters Tel Aviv University professor Anson Rainey. He believes the Israelites may be identified with the pastoralist people known as the Shasu, the figures shown wearing knee-length skirts above (drawing below). The Israelites, then, may not have emerged out of Canaanite society at all but rather crystallized from wandering shepherds from outside of Canaan. In Rainey's view the reason the figures on the previous page look like Canaanites is that they* are *Canaanites, illustrating the line "Canaan has been plundered into every sort of woe."* Photo by Frank Yurco. Drawing by F. Schonbach.

Canaan and Kharu, from which the versification was developed. This included Israel, which was contained within Canaan entirely. Egyptian texts coming from the political milieu, whether poetic or not, must be considered within the framework of Egyptian political administration and organization. The poetry should reflect the political reality, not, as Bimson would have it, the other way around.[23] By splitting Israel off from Canaan, Bimson overgauges its importance and upsets the symmetry between the Merenptah text and the political structures of the provinces of Canaan and Kharu, a structure also reflected in Merenptah's campaign reliefs at Karnak with the battles in sequence. Ahlström and Bimson both have distorted this symmetry with their proposed versification, intended to give Israel a special emphasis.

The final concern in this discussion centers on the Shasu. They are found in Merenptah's battle reliefs only in the prisoner-binding scene and in the victory march back to Egypt with the prisoners.[24] There is no mention of Shasu in the "Israel" Stela, nor are they represented in any of the four battle scenes, contra Redford's claim. This probably reflects their minor role within the context of Merenptah's Canaanite campaign. Yet the fact that they are named Shasu in the inscriptions accompanying the scenes in which they are represented makes it certain that Merenptah did not view them as Israel, despite the claims of many.[25] Shasu are found in Egyptian battle reliefs and other texts throughout the New Kingdom, from Thutmose III to the Third Intermediate Period, and typically play a harassing role, nettling the Egyptian campaigns bound for Canaan or Syria. For this, the Egyptians punished them regularly. Papyrus Anastasi I views them in exactly the same light, and it has them speaking a Semitic language.[26] Nowhere, however, do the Egyptians call the Shasu Israelites. Thus, despite the queries, Merenptah's fourth battle scene at Karnak remains the one that depicts Israel. Israelites, as Merenptah saw them, resembled the Canaanites most closely. Nevertheless, based on the account of Deborah (Judges 5:15-16), some of the Israelites were pastoralists; they perhaps originated as Shasu, while others seem to have originated among the Sea Peoples (as some scholars have proposed regarding the tribe of Dan, because Dan was "on ships" when Deborah called for help against Megiddo).[27] Thus all the major population groups found in 13th- to 12th-century B.C.E. Canaan—Canaanites, Shasu, and Sea Peoples—probably had a role in the development of Israel as a state.

Bimson justifiably argues that many theories about Israelite origins should be harmonized chronologically and structurally to reflect Merenptah's Canaanite campaign as well as other Egyptian evidence regarding Canaan and early Israel. Too many recent studies have failed to take account adequately of such Egyptian evidence.[28] Without considering these Egyptian sources, any study of Israel's early origins cannot be complete.

In the most basic analysis, the Merenptah Canaanite reliefs and other Egyptian sources suggest the following developments. Papyrus Anastasi I indicates no substantial Israelite or other settlement in the hill country of Canaan as of its date (about the middle of Ramesses II's reign, c. 1250 B.C.E.); settlement of Canaan's hill country commenced only after this time. By the time of Merenptah's second to third regnal year (1210-1209 B.C.E.), however, substantial settlement was underway in the hill country as confirmed by Stager's excavations. Stager identified these new settlers as Israelites, and Merenptah's "Israel" Stela and Canaanite battle reliefs confirm this, naming Israel for the first time in an Egyptian or any other extra-biblical source. Merenptah's Canaanite reliefs indicate that the Israelites he encountered were very similar to the Canaanites of the cities and not at all like Shasu. Consequently, part of early Israel may derive from the Canaanite population. According to the Papyrus Anastasi I, however, Shasu were found in the hill country, and Merenptah encountered them in his Canaanite campaign, as indicated in his reliefs, but they were a minor factor not reflected in the larger picture shown in the "Israel" Stela. Papyrus Anastasi I, moreover, depicts the Shasu as Semitic-language speakers. Deborah's text (Judges 5:15-16) depicts some Israelites as pastoralists, and these might have originated among the Shasu, especially as other Egyptian documents do show certain Shasu as pastoralists. Also, the deity Yahweh may originate from Edomite Shasu peoples.[29]

Merenptah's campaign thwarted the early expansion efforts of the early Israelites. He strengthened Egyptian rule over Canaan and, coupled with Ramesses III's early efforts, kept Israel out of the lowlands and coastal areas of Canaan. Following his eighth regnal year, Ramesses III, however, allowed the Sea Peoples who attacked him en masse, including the Peleset (Philistines), Tjekker (Shiqalaya), and some Sherden and Danuna, to settle, initially under his control; but soon thereafter, de facto, they became independent. In the interior parts of Canaan, Egyptian control lasted, at latest, to Ramesses VI's reign. After the Egyptian evacuation, Israel was at last able to descend into the lowlands and defeat the Canaanites, as the Song of Deborah indicates. The Canaanites had been weakened by the loss of Egyptian support and by their losses to the Sea Peoples now settled in Canaan. This corroborates dating the song to just after Ramesses VI (c. 1133 B.C.E.). The Song of Deborah also depicts the Israelites as a very disparate group, still fractured and not yet unified into the later twelve-tribe structure. The song also indicates the disparate origins of the Israelites—some Canaanite, some of Shasu origin, and even some of Sea Peoples' origin.

How does all this Egyptian data and Merenptah's campaign and reference to Israel relate to the question of the Exodus as recorded in the Old Testament? There is very little direct relevance, but for those who allow at least some historicity to the Exodus story, it does represent a *terminus ante quem*. Another point is that Merenptah's recording of Israel, Yisrael to be precise, agrees exactly with the spelling and sound of the biblical name that now comes to be used for *Bene Yisrael*. As previously suggested, even the Egyptian pronoun ·f (his), referring back to Yisrael in the "Israel" Stela's phrase bn prt·f, seems to accord with the Israelites' recognition that the name Yisrael originates with an eponymous ancestor, Jacob, who came to be called Yisrael.[30]

Turning to the Exodus narrative itself, several points are worth noting. First, for those who doubt the historicity of the story completely, or who suggest that it was created only in the sixth to fifth century B.C.E. post-Exilic era, a question must be asked regarding Ramesses and Pithom, the cities on which the Hebrews labored, according to Exodus.[31] Why did the biblical editors or redactors refer specifically to Ramesses, when in their own era and for some three centuries earlier the capital of Egypt had been Tanis, a city well known and often referred to in the Old Testament? From the Book of Judges onwards, Tanis is consistently referred to as Egypt's capital. Why would a biblical editor insert Ramesses into a newly composed story when that city no longer existed in Egypt and had not been Pharaoh's residence or the capital for the previous four to five centuries? This particularly is troublesome if, as Redford claims, the Exodus account is entirely a folk tale, fabricated in the post-Exilic period.[32] Tanis, Bubastis, and other Late Period delta cities were built out of the ruins of Per-Ramesses and other Ramesside-era cities; Tanis had been the Egyptian capital throughout nearly the entire span of Israel's monarchic period. What sense would it make for Jews familiar with Saite Egypt to invent a story about an oppressive pharaoh who had compelled their ancestors to labor on his cities, and why fix on Ramesses for this role? In Dynasty XXVI Pharaoh's capital was Sais, and even more pointedly, Jewish exiles in Egypt were valued for their mercenary skills and not consigned to compulsory brick making. In light of this, the selection of Ramesses in the Exodus story is an enigma, unless some ancestral memory of Ramesside Egypt did survive among the Jews in Egypt in the Saite era. Picking the name and city of Ramesses in the Late Period for the Exodus story makes no sense unless there were some ancestral memory of some event that really had happened in the Ramesside era, when Per-Ramesses was the capital and residence of Pharaoh. Without such a memory, why would even the existence of cults of Ramesses of Tanis or Ramesses of Bubastis mean anything to the Saite era Jewish exiles in Egypt?[33]

In fact, two very old segments of poetic text, one from Exodus and one from Judges, suggest that some parts of the biblical story do indeed date back to the 13th to 12th centuries B.C.E. These are the Song of Moses and the Children of Israel and the Song of Deborah the Judge.[34] Both are composed in very archaic Hebrew, and most scholars of biblical texts agree on a date in the 13th- to 12th-century B.C.E. time frame.[35] Also, as shown above, the Song of Deborah accurately reflects the splintered entity of disparate origins that Israel was in the mid to late 12th century B.C.E., an analysis that Lawrence Stager agrees with.[36] The Song of Moses and the Children of Israel and Miriam describes a miraculous departure from Egypt. It seems to be the one piece of authentic tradition, albeit poetic, surviving from the 13th century B.C.E. that ties the event to the Ramesside era. The fleeing Hebrews perhaps crossed a *yam sûf* (*yam chuf* in Egyptian), a papyrus-filled marshy lake; this is hinted at by a verse in Exodus.[37] So rather than a miracle of the sea, this fragment of text may show a trace of an original story of a real escape; one that is classic, used by slaves escaping in other cultures also. Pursuit through a marsh, papyrus or otherwise, would prove difficult, especially with chariots.[38] Could this possibly preserve a trace of the original Exodus story, interpolated into the miraculous in the later redactions? It would also make sense of the reference to *yam chuf* as the body of water that was crossed, with no need to emend that into the Red Sea. While the Exodus story does not name the pharaoh, it does record him by one of two cities that the Hebrews were made to labor on, namely, Ramesses,[39] or Per-Ramesses, as it was known in Ramesside Egypt.[40]

From what is known of Ramesses II's reign, it is clear that this pharaoh did not hesitate to press foreign peoples into his labor battalions. Ramesses II also outdid all other pharaohs, before or after, in the scale of his building operations. Ramesside documents mention ʿpiru laboring on the monuments of Per-Ramesses and Memphis.[41] This pharaoh also had his viceroy of Kush round up Tjemeh-Libyans in a raid in Nubia, in regnal year 44, whom he employed to build the Wady es-Sebua temple.[42] In his wide-ranging building projects, Ramesses II also built actual store-cities, for military supplies, in the Egyptian delta, along with substantially enlarging and rebuilding Per-Ramesses and turning it into his capital.[43] The city was thus vastly enlarged from its modest beginnings under Horemheb and Sety I[44] (likewise, this pattern of more than one pharaoh working on the project also matches the Exodus story). Aside from temples, normally built of stone in this era, palaces, storehouses, temple auxiliary and out-buildings, and residences for military personnel and administrators were all constructed of mudbricks. As was traditional in Egypt, labor for these projects was recruited from the people in the area. Millions of mudbricks would have been required for such projects, and this is exactly the type of work the Exodus story says the Hebrews were forced to do. Also significant is the difference in treatment Ramesses II accorded indigenous Egyptians employed on building projects, contrasted with foreigners conscripted for such work.[45] Further, the milieu of the Exodus story, with Moses and Aaron making daily visits to Pharaoh, makes sense only in the Ramesside era when Pharaoh was resident in Per-Ramesses. It is an obstacle for those who advocate an XVIIIth Dynasty date for the Exodus, as Pharaoh was resident in Memphis at that time; and Memphis was a three-day voyage by river from Per-Ramesses.[46] Likewise, in Dynasty XXVI Pharaoh's capital was Sais, and moreover, in the Saite era Jews in Egypt were not employed as conscripted labor for building projects but were highly valued mercenaries. In addition, the Exodus account contains personal names—Moses, Phineas, Hophni, Shiprah, and Puah—that are charac-

Pharaoh's Firstborn. *This hieroglyphic inscription from a recently discovered tomb in the Valley of Kings bears the name of Ramesses II's firstborn son, Amun-her-khepesh-ef. Based on ancient Egyptian references, Frank Yurco estimates that the crown prince perished sometime between his father's 20th and 30th regnal years, about 1259-1249 B.C.E. Ramesses II is a likely candidate for the role of pharaoh of the Exodus, if indeed there was a historical Exodus; Amun-her-khepesh-ef, therefore, would have been the hapless offspring struck down in the final plague, the death of the firstborn sons.* Photo by Kent Weeks.

teristic of the Ramesside era, less so in Dynasty XVIII and least of all in Dynasty XXVI. In Egyptian the names Moses and Phineas (Mose and Panehsy) are found frequently in Ramesside sources as personal names.[47] Thus, as Dever stated in the symposium, *Exodus' Sitz im Leben* suits the Ramesside age in Egypt admirably.[48]

Can any other evidence be adduced from Egypt that supports dating the Exodus story to the Ramesside age? In Exodus it states that in the final plague sent against Pharaoh by God all the firstborn males in Egypt, from Pharaoh's son to that of the lowliest peasant, all perished.[49] If Ramesses II is a prime candidate for the Exodus date, when did he lose his eldest son and crown prince Amun-her-khepesh-ef, attested as

Ramesses II's eldest son and born to Queen Nofretari?[50] He also is represented as crown prince at Abydos, in Sety I's temple in Ramesses II's reliefs; and his latest attestation may be from correspondence between the Egyptian and Hittite courts after the peace treaty between Ramesses II and Hattusilis III of regnal year 21, or it may perhaps be some years later.[51] Certainly it was by regnal year 30, for by then Queen Isis-nofret's children had secured the positions of crown prince and high priest of Ptah.[52] Khaemwast, the high priest of Ptah, had rock-inscribed texts carved to announce Pharaoh's first jubilee. These texts also document his brother's tenure as the crown prince and other high titles for other of his siblings. Thus it may be estimated that Amun-her-khepesh-ef, Ramesses II's eldest son, perished between about regnal year 20 and 30, that is, 1259-1249 B.C.E., following Kitchen's dating for the Ramesside era; an exodus event at this date would fit well with the *terminus ante quem* indicated by Merenptah's reference to Israel in Canaan, and it also agrees well with Papyrus Anastasi I.

This is as far as the Egyptian indirect evidence goes, and it has drawn the support of Kitchen, the foremost Ramesside scholar.[53] Still, several further observations regarding the biblical data are in order. Many people focus on the 480 years (12 generations of 40 years each, by biblical reckoning) that passed between the Exodus and Solomon's building of the temple in Jerusalem. Yet anthropologists usually allow about 25 years for a generation, and the Egyptian text *Teaching for Merikare*, a IXth to Xth Dynasty composition, sets 20 years as the time for generational replacement.[54] If the 12 biblical generations are refigured at 20-25 years each, the result is 240 to 300 years as the time elapsed between the Exodus and the building of Solomon's temple. Solomon's reign is set at 962 to 922 B.C.E. by cross references to Dynasty XXI and working back from Israelite-Assyrian synchronisms.[55] Working back from Solomon's 4th regnal year, 958 B.C.E., the Exodus would fall between 1198 to 1258 B.C.E., with the upper limit well within Ramesses II's reign around the 21st regnal year.

This would also agree with the dating of the two poetic texts in Exodus and Judges.[56]

As for the number of Israelites said to have left Egypt in the Exodus, 600,000 clearly is inflated highly. If *Bene Yisrael* initially included only the descendents of Jacob, then 6,000, or even 600, would be a more reasonable figure. Such a group might easily have escaped through a swampy or marshy papyrus lake and then via the southern route through the Sinai, and such a group would have had plenty to fear from the Egyptian garrisons stationed along the Way of Horus, anachronistically called the Way of the Philistines.[57] According to the Exodus story, initially the Israelites had permission to leave. Once Pharaoh changed his mind and decided to pursue them, the thoroughness of the border policing becomes evident,[58] as shown with the two slaves mentioned in a late XIXth Dynasty text, in flight and pursued by Egyptian authorities.[59]

A smaller group, as discussed above, would leave little trace of their passing and also wouldn't overtax the resources of the Sinai. Yet if they carried the tradition of the sojourn in Egypt, the oppression by Pharaoh, and the winning of their freedom, they could have passed on these events as a foundation story to the disparate populations that later came to constitute historic Israel.[60] Merenptah and Ramesses III delayed the emergence of the new nation until after the Egyptians evacuated Canaan in 1141 to 1133 B.C.E., the time of Deborah the judge.[61] By allowing the Philistines and Tjekker and other Sea Peoples to settle along the Canaanite coast, Ramesses III simply exchanged the Egyptian nemesis for the Philistine nemesis that confounded the Israelites in the Book of Judges.

No other theory about the Exodus, dated to different periods, associates so well with the emerging archaeological evidence of the earliest Israelite settlement in Canaan, the circumstantial evidence from Egyptian data, and the one precise reference to Israel in Canaan from Merenptah's "Israel" Stela and the Canaanite campaign reliefs—all of which occur within the 13th century B.C.E. That the Exodus story doesn't mention Pharaoh's name is not unusual. In Egyptian administrative documents Pharaoh's name is often omitted and only a regnal date given. This would especially be true with a long-reigning king like Ramesses II. Yet, in recalling that they labored on Ramesses and Pithom, the Israelites preserved the name of the pharaoh of the Exodus. It was Ramesses II himself who named his new capital Per-Ramesses, and Pithom, as Per-Atum, is also named in a Ramesside text.[62]

In conclusion, the biblical account preserves two short poetic sections of text that date the root of the Exodus story to the Ramesside era, and the milieu of Ramesses II's Egypt is a period that offers considerable indirect supporting evidence for the event. As most scholars now agree, the biblical account was reworked many times, most recently in the sixth to fifth century B.C.E.[63] With Redford and Bietak I would agree that Jewish refugees living in Egypt as exiles after 586 B.C.E came looking for monuments relating to their received traditions of the Exodus. They were misled by the destruction of the Ramesside sites, by the relocation of stonework from these sites to newer Saite construction, and by surviving cults of Ramesses of Tanis and Ramesses of Bubastis. While they have added some details of Saite Egypt to the story, respect for the received tradition resulted in the preservation of significant details of the original account, the personal names in Exodus, and the names of the cities their ancestors had labored on, under a demanding and oppressive pharaoh.[64] Those details plus the antiquity of Exodus 15 and Judges 5 provide anchors for dating the original Exodus event and the withdrawal of the Egyptians from Canaan, which finally allowed Israel to begin coalescing into a nation-state. The Canaanite campaign reliefs of Merenptah and other Egyptian evidence, such as Papyrus Anastasi I and other documents cited, provide a background for the period in which early Israel evolved, despite conflicts with the Sea Peoples whom Ramesses III had allowed to settle in coastal Canaan. Recent archaeological work by Stager

and others increasingly adds to this picture of Israel emerging in the 13th-
to 12th-century B.C.E. period.[65]

ENDNOTES

[1] John J. Bimson, "Merneptah's Israel and Recent Theories of Israelite Origins," *Journal For the Study of the Old Testament* 49 (1991), pp. 3-29.

[2] Frank J. Yurco, "Merenptah's Canaanite Campaign," *Journal of the American Research Center in Egypt* 23 (1986), pp. 189-215; and "3,200-Year-Old Pictures of Israelites Found in Egypt," *Biblical Archaeology Review* 16:5 (1990), pp. 20-38.

[3] Donald B. Redford, "The Ashkelon Relief at Karnak and the Israel Stele," *Israel Exploration Journal* 36 (1986), pp. 188-200; and *Egypt, Canaan, and Israel in Ancient Times* (Princeton: Princeton University Press, 1992), p. 275, esp. n. 85.

[4] Yurco, "Once Again, Merenptah's Battle Reliefs at Karnak," *Israel Exploration Journal* (forthcoming).

[5] Redford, "Ashkelon Relief," p. 193; but see Yurco, "Merenptah's Canaanite Campaign," pp. 196-199, figs. 10-11, p. 25, illustrations, and inset, and "Once Again." Note also Kenneth Kitchen, *Pharaoh Triumphant: The Life and Times of Ramesses II* (Mississauga: Benben, 1982), p. 220, and *Ramesside Inscriptions, Historical and Biographical*, 7 vols. (Oxford, 1968-), vol. 4, p. 82, as well as the support of other Egyptologists, including Dr. Schulman at this symposium.

[6] Yurco, "Merenptah's Canaanite Campaign," p. 193, fig. 5, pp. 32-33, illustrations.

[7] Anson Rainey, "Can You Name the Panel with the Israelites?" *Biblical Archaeology Review* 17:6 (1991), pp. 56-60, 93; and my response, p. 61. It is worth noting that Rainey, too, accepts my identification of these reliefs as Merenptah's.

[8] Bimson, "Merneptah's Israel," p. 23 and n. 1.

[9] The most recent treatment is Edward F. Wente, *Letters From Ancient Egypt*, ed. Edmund S. Meltzer (Atlanta: Scholars Press, 1990), pp. 98-110.

[10] See William Murnane, *The Road to Kadesh*, 2d rev. ed., Studies in Ancient Oriental Civilizations 42 (Chicago: Oriental Institute, 1990), pp. 42-43; Yohanan Aharoni, *The Land of the Bible*, 2d ed. (Philadelphia: Westminster Press, 1979), p. 12, map; and Redford, *Egypt*, p. 292.

[11] Lawrence Stager, "The Archeology of the Family in Ancient Israel," *Bulletin of the American Schools of Oriental Research* 260 (November 1985), pp. 1-35.

[12] Yurco, "Merenptah's Canaanite Campaign," pp. 211-213.

[13] Yurco, "Merenptah's Canaanite Campaign," pp. 214-215.

[14] Eliezer D. Oren, "'Governors' Residences' in Canaan Under the New Kingdom: A Case Study of Egyptian Administration," *Journal of the Society for the Study of Egyptian Antiquities* 14:2 (1984), pp. 37-56; see also Orly Goldwasser, "The Lachish Bowl, Once Again," *Tel Aviv* 9 (1982), pp. 137-138.

[15] Judges 4-5; Stager, "The Song of Deborah: Why Some Tribes Answered the Call and Others Did Not," *Biblical Archaeology Review* 15:1 (1989), pp. 50-64.

[16] See Yurco, "Merenptah's Canaanite Campaign," pp. 214-215; also Trude Dothan and Moshe Dothan, *People of the Sea: The Search for the Philistines* (New York: Macmillan, 1992), pp. 212-213. Shardana were active in the eastern Mediterranean earlier and even served as Egyptian mercenaries after being captured. See Kitchen, *Inscriptions*, vol. 2, p. 290, no. 2, and *Pharaoh Triumphant*, pp. 40-41. Such Sea Peoples earlier on could account for the situation at Akko.

[17] Papyrus Harris, see James B. Pritchard, ed., *Ancient Near Eastern Texts Relating to the Old Testament*, 3d ed. (Princeton: Princeton University Press, 1969), p. 262.

[18] For instance, the triumphal scene at the Karnak temple, Second Pylon (in Kitchen, *Inscriptions*, vol. 6, p. 284, no. 12), the Cairo Museum statue (p. 286, no. 13), and the Ramesses VI statue base from Megiddo (p. 278); see also Redford, *Egypt*, pp. 290-292.

[19] 1 Samuel 13:19-22, though doubted by Aharoni (*Land of the Bible*, p. 274). Even if this doubt is correct, the Philistines enjoyed other material advantages over the early Israelites; see T. Dothan and M. Dothan, *People of the Sea*, pp. 99-106, 172-174, 250, 259.

[20] Bimson, "Merenptah's Israel," p. 20 n. 1.

[21] Kitchen, *Inscriptions*, vol. 4, p. 5, line 3 (line 24 of text); p. 24, no. 7A. Claude Schaeffer, "Les fouilles de Ras Shamra-Ugarit," *Annales Archéologiques de Syrie* 3 (1953), pp. 141-142 and fig. 15.

[22] Yurco, "Merenptah's Canaanite Campaign," pp. 210-211.

[23] Bimson, "Merenptah's Israel," pp. 20-21, esp. p. 20 n. 1.

[24] Yurco, "Merenptah's Canaanite Campaign," pp. 209-210, figs. 6, 8, 9; Redford (*Egypt*, p. 275) claims that in the Ashkelon scene Shasu captives are shown being led away as prisoners; this, patently, is wrong! Shasu in Merenptah's reliefs are seen only in the prisoner binding scene (scene 5 in my article) and in the scenes of return to Egypt with all prisoners, Canaanites and Shasu. Ashkelon and the other fortresses are held and defended strictly by Canaanites, and scene 4, Israel by my analysis, also has only Canaanite-type people. See Yurco, "Merenptah's Canaanite Campaign," pp. 192-193, figs. 2, 3, 4, 5, contrasted with pp. 194-195, figs. 6, 8, 9, and pp. 29-33, illustrations, as contrasted with p. 35. One cannot help but wonder if Redford has ever looked at this wall in person or even looked closely at photographs in my articles.

[25] See, for example, Raphael Giveon, *Les Bedouins Shosou* (Leiden: Brill, 1972); also Redford, *Egypt*, pp. 275-280. Merenptah's campaign reliefs as well as the Song of Deborah (Judges 4-5) refute the view of Israel originating from one single group of the Canaanite population. See Stager, "Song of Deborah," pp. 50-64.

[26] Wente, *Letters From Ancient Egypt*, pp. 98-110, esp. 106; also Redford, *Egypt*, pp. 271-274.

[27] Judges 5:15-17; also Yigael Yadin, "And Dan, Why Did He Abide by the Ships?" *Australian Journal of Archaeology* 1 (1968), pp. 9-23; and T. Dothan and M. Dothan, *People of the Sea*, pp. 215-219. For the Shasu component, see Judges 5:16 and Redford, *Egypt*, pp. 272-280. Redford's analysis of Yahweh originating from Se'ir's (Edom) population of Shasu (esp. p. 272 n. 72, following R. de Vaux, Lepinski, and Axelssohn), particularly, is attractive.

[28] Bimson, "Merenptah's Israel," pp. 16-20. For two other, even more recent, examples, see Manfred Weippert and Helga Weippert, "Die vorgeschichte Israels in neuem Licht," *Theologische Rundschau* 56 (1991), pp. 341-390, esp. 344-345, with hardly a mention of

Merenptah's campaign; and Marit Skjeggestad, "Ethnic Groups in Early Iron Age Palestine: Some Remarks on the Use of the Term 'Israelite' in Recent Research," *Scandinavian Journal of the Old Testament* 6 (1992), pp. 159-186, esp. 166 n. 18. By depending only on Redford's study, Skjeggestad falls into the trap of equating Israel with Shasu, something that Merenptah's battle reliefs contradict but that she missed, just as she also missed Papyrus Anastasi I, Kitchen's references, and the Song of Deborah, all with indications of early Israel's diversity.

[29] See Judges 5:4; also Redford, *Egypt*, p. 273 n. 72 and references therein.

[30] Yurco, "Merenptah's Canaanite Campaign," pp. 211, 190 n. 3; also Genesis 34:10.

[31] Exodus 1:11, 12:37.

[32] Redford, *Egypt*, pp. 257-263; also Gösta Ahlström, *Who Were the Israelites?* (Winona Lake, IN: Eisenbrauns, 1986), pp. 44-55.

[33] Manfred Bietak, *Avaris and Piramesse: Archaeological Exploration in the Eastern Nile Delta*, Proceedings of the British Academy, London 65 (Oxford: Oxford University Press, 1979), pp. 278-279.

[34] Exodus 15 and Judges 5. Even Redford (*Egypt*, p. 412 n. 89) accepts these texts as authentic surviving examples of early Israelite tradition, though, following Ahlström, he dates them later than the 13th to 12th century B.C.E.

[35] See Frank Cross, *Canaanite Myth and Hebrew Epic* (Cambridge, MA: Cambridge University Press, 1973), pp. 121-125; and David Noel Freedman, "Early Israelite History in the Light of Early Israelite Poetry," in *Unity and Diversity: Essays in History, Literature, and Religion of the Ancient Near East*, ed. Hans Goedicke and J.J.M. Roberts (Baltimore: Johns Hopkins University Press, 1975), pp. 3-23.

[36] Stager, "Song of Deborah," pp. 50-64.

[37] Exodus 14:25; Ricardo Caminos (*Late Egyptian Miscellanies* [London: Oxford University Press, 1954], pp. 74, 79) identifies Egyptian P3-twf with biblical *Yam sûph*. The Egyptian means "papyrus marsh"; one such swampy, marshy lake was located near the Ramesside capital, and the eastern delta had several such sweet-water papyrus marshy lakes. See, too, John H. Stek, "What Happened to the Chariot Wheels of Exod 14.25?" *Journal of Biblical Literature* 105:2 (1986), pp. 293-294.

[38] Bernard Batto ("Red Sea or Reed Sea?" *Biblical Archaeology Review* 10:4 [1984], p. 62) noted that Exodus 14:25 is a surviving bit of a variant E author's Exodus account, while the rest, the P-author narrative, is the miraculous sea partition. Exodus 14:25, which mentions chariot wheels clogging, exactly describes what would happen to a chariot driven through a papyrus swamp; see Stek, "Exod 14:25," pp. 293-294. As known from American 19th-century slave escape stories, swamps were the escape route of choice, where pursuers found it hard to track and follow. Thus the E fragment (Exodus 14:25) plus the original *Yam sûph* (from Egyptian "papyrus marsh"; Exodus 15:4) may be part of a factual account. Mingling facts and miracles is known from other biblical texts, e.g., the story of Deborah in Judges 4-5. As Exodus 15 is original, 13th-century B.C.E. poetry (see n. 35, above), Numbers 33:8 and 10 perhaps had interchanged the references to *Yam sûph*, and this could account for later *Yam sûph*-Red Sea references.

[39] Exodus 1:11, 12:27.

[40] Bietak, *Avaris and Piramesse*, pp. 230, 279-283.

[41] Caminos, *Late Egyptian Miscellanies*, p. 491 (Papyrus Leiden, 348, v. 6,5 to 7,1); also Wente, *Letters from Ancient Egypt*, pp. 123-124 (Papyrus Leiden I, 349).

[42] Kitchen, *Pharaoh Triumphant*, pp. 70-71, 138.

[43] Kitchen, *Pharaoh Triumphant*, pp. 70-71, 119-123. This clearly contradicts Redford, *Egypt*, p. 416. First, Ramesses II's military delta cities and forts can be described as "store-cities," for they were where this pharaoh's military supplies were kept in readiness for campaigns in Syria-Palestine. Second, mudbricks were far more in demand than stonework, the latter being used only for temples, and last, Ramesses II was notorious for impressing foreigners to labor on his building projects, as discussed in nn. 41-42, above.

[44] Bietak, *Avaris and Piramesse*, pp. 229-231, 268-272; Kitchen, *Pharaoh Triumphant*, p. 119.

[45] Cf. Kitchen, *Pharaoh Triumphant*, pp. 120, 138, and *The Bible in Its World* (Exeter: PaterNoster Press, 1977), pp. 77-78, for brick quotas demanded under Ramesses II.

[46] See Eric P. Uphill, "Pithom and Raamses: Their Location and Significance," *Journal of Near Eastern Studies* 28 (1969), p. 21, from a Ramesside text.

[47] The personal names are hardest to reconcile with a XXVIth Dynasty date of composition of the Exodus story, as Redford (*Egypt*, p. 418 and n. 119) admits. This contrasts sharply with the Genesis story of Joseph, which as Redford (pp. 422-429) proposes, was composed in the time of Dynasty XXVI or else was revised extensively at that time.

[48] William Dever, see his paper presented at this symposium.

[49] Exodus 12:29; Kitchen, *Pharaoh Triumphant*, pp. 70-71.

[50] Kitchen, *Pharaoh Triumphant*, pp. 70-71.

[51] Kitchen, *Pharaoh Triumphant*, p. 80; the prince in the Hittite correspondence is Seth-her-khepesh-ef, and unless this is yet another name for Amun-her-khepesh-ef, it represents Queen Nofretari's younger son, and Amun-her-khepesh-ef died earlier in the reign.

[52] Kitchen, *Pharaoh Triumphant*, pp. 100, 103.

[53] Kitchen, *Pharaoh Triumphant*, pp. 70-71; and *The Bible in Its World*, pp. 75-79.

[54] Miriam Lichtheim, *Ancient Egyptian Literature*, vol. 1 (Berkeley: University of California Press, 1973), p. 101; Redford (*Egypt*, pp. 259-260) criticizes such recalculation, but in light of Merykare, the biblical 40 years, clearly, is too long, and 20-25 years per generation would be more reasonable—provided it is applied consistently. Of course, individuals did survive longer, Ramesses II providing a perfect example, or earlier, the incredibly long-lived Pepy II. Genesis 50:26 gives Joseph an age of 110 years at death, a figure reflecting, perhaps, the Egyptian ideal of old age survival. Countering Redford's utter skepticism of the biblical record and efforts to integrate it into ancient Near Eastern history, see Kitchen, review of *Egypt*, by Redford, in *Biblical Archaeology Review* 19:1 (1993), pp. 6-8; and *The Bible in Its World*, esp. pp. 56-74, 75-91.

[55] 1 Kings 6:1; 2 Chronicles 3:2. Also *Interpreters' Dictionary of the Bible* (Nashville: Abingdon Press, 1962), vol. 4, pp. 399-404.

[56] See Cross, *Canaanite Myth and Hebrew Epic*, pp. 121-125; Freedman, "Early Israelite Poetry."

[57] Exodus 13:17.

[58] Papyrus Anastasi III, in Caminos, *Late Egyptian Miscellanies*, pp. 108-109, and Anastasi VI, p. 293.

[59] Papyrus Anastasi V, in Caminos, *Late Egyptian Miscellanies*, p. 255; as Kitchen (*The Bible in Its World*, p. 78) notes, this was precisely the same route used in Exodus 12:37 by the

fleeing Israelites, again contradicting Redford's claim of few Ramesside details in the Exodus story (see *Egypt*, pp. 408-413).

[60] Ahlström (*Who Were the Israelites?* p. 46) allows the possibility of such a transmission. Still, his idea that it reflects the Hyksos expulsion is ruled out by the dating of Exodus 15 to the 13th century B.C.E., right in the Ramesside era (see n. 35, above).

[61] On dating the Egyptian withdrawal from Canaan there is strong agreement, see Redford, *Egypt*, pp. 290-293; Stager, "Song of Deborah," pp. 50-64; Kitchen, *The Bible in Its World*, p. 91; and T. Dothan and M. Dothan, *People of the Sea*, pp. 103-104; and n. 18, above.

[62] Papyrus Anastasi VI, 56-58, see Caminos, *Late Egyptian Miscellanies*, pp. 293-295. This reference is to a Ramesside Pithom, specifically, "pools of Pr-Atum of Merenptah which are in Tjeku nome." While Tell el-Maskhuta has only Saite remains (contra Redford, *Egypt*, p. 451 n. 92), there are Ramesside era remains at Tell er-Ratabeh, and that is the Ramesside Pithom (see Redford, "Pithom," in *Lexikon der Ägyptologie*, 6 vols. [Wiesbaden: Harrassowitz, 1972-1986], vol. 4, pp. 1,054-1,058). As in the case of Per-Ramesses and Tanis, Ramesside Pithom's ruins were used to build Saite Pithom, again causing confusion for Jewish visitors in the Late Period seeking the Pithom of their tradition.

[63] Even Redford (*Egypt*, p. 412 n. 89) allows that an ancient tradition of Israel coming out of Egypt may have survived, based on Exodus 15 and references in some of the psalms. While relocation of Ramesside cities may have caused some confusion for Saite era Jews, even to the point of Psalm 78:12-13 setting the Exodus event in Zoan (Tanis), it is all the more remarkable that the Exodus story itself wasn't harmonized and altered to say that the Israelites in Egypt labored on Tanis and not Per-Ramesses.

[64] Certainly nothing that happened to Jewish exiles in Saite Egypt, where they were valued as mercenaries, matches the oppressive pharaoh of Exodus.

[65] A book that appeared too recently to be integrated fully, Hershel Shanks, William G. Dever, Baruch Halpern, and P. Kyle McCarter, Jr., *The Rise of Ancient Israel* (Washington, DC: Biblical Archaeology Society, 1992), contains valuable supporting data for my positions stated above, including further historical support for Merenptah's Canaanite campaign (pp. 154-157) and support for the view that the earliest Israelites emerged in the time after Papyrus Anastasi I, in the latter half of Ramesses II's reign (pp. 144-145), and that they were a disparate grouping of farmers, pastoralists, and traders of Canaanite, Shasu, and perhaps Sea Peoples origin (Dever, pp. 27-56), and even allows the possibility of an Exodus event (Halpern, pp. 87-113).

3

OBSERVATIONS ON THE SOJOURN OF THE BENE-ISRAEL

Donald B. Redford

"Coming out" implies a previous "being in," of however short or long a duration, and while the Miracle at the Sea, the Wanderings, and the Conquest are discrete foci of Pentateuchal tradition,[1] the Exodus cannot be considered without examining the Sojourn. Yet in many ways, especially historically, the Sojourn must be viewed in isolation from the material in Exodus 12 onward, for the settlement of ethnic elements from Asia in parts of the delta and the Nile Valley is a common demographic phenomenon from the earliest times. And the interaction of Semitic-speaking communities from the Levant with the autochthonous inhabitants of the Nile Valley presents us with too complicated, yet significant, a picture to be passed over cavalierly or ignored.

We must distinguish the varying dynamics of this interaction between Egypt and the foreign community on the basis of a number of variables: motivation for moving into Egypt, means (coercive or voluntary) of getting there, size of community, social class to which its members belonged,

livelihood and activity in Egypt, length of stay, and so forth. The evidence
will thus enable us to elicit several different types of sojourn.

There is, for example, the kind of resident sojourner who is the product of commercial intercourse, in which Egypt usually had the whip
hand. The House of Ba'al of Mennofre,[2] the Camp of the Milesians,[3] the
Shasu of Atfih,[4] the House of the Southern Shasu,[5] the Fort of the Syrian[6]
and the Harbor-House[7] are examples of colonies of foreign merchants
who settled in Egypt with Egyptian permission or acquiescence to do
business with the natives. It is highly likely that the Aramean enclaves at
Elephantine and Migdol, although functioning garrisons, also engaged
in commerce.[8] The members of such communities, although obliged to
meet with Egyptians in the marketplace, retained their individuality as
a group. Archaeologically, the record would vary considerably, depending on the frequency of the contacts between the colony and its home-
land (not to mention such unmeasurables as predilection, social status,
relations with authorities, etc.). But it might be ill advised, solely on the
basis of artifactual or ceramic percentages, for example, to speak of varying degrees of acclimation unless we have specific textual evidence.[9]

In assessing the impact these merchant settlements had on Egypt
during the New Kingdom, one usually trots out the archaeological
record, but a perhaps greater influence is to be inferred from the practice
of the Egyptian marketplace "to do business in the tongue of Syria."[10] It
is, in fact, the lexicon that betrays the extent of Canaanite penetration
into Egyptian culture and not the ceramic repertoire. One might even
say that here (as elsewhere) a word is worth a thousand pots.

Hundreds of words from Western Asia (mainly, though by no means
exclusively, "Canaanite") turn up in Late Egyptian transcribed in syl-
labic orthography. Although the Egyptian language, for the most part,
resisted change in the realm of syntax and grammar, clearly the need
for terms for new techniques, materials, and manufactures resulted in a
foreign vocabulary (though not, technically speaking, loan words) that

is impressive indeed. As one might expect, fully one-quarter of those terms identified have to do with the military (chariots, weapons, ranks, military architecture, and methods of warfare). Egyptian familiarity with Asia accounts for another quarter. Terms for wood, lumber, and types of furniture amount to 12 percent, while 6 percent covers minerals. Geographical terms amount to approximately 12 percent of the total (of which over half designate bodies of water). The remainder of the terms illustrates what archaeological and historical evidence has already shown us. Food and its preparation account for 8 percent of foreign words, while construction techniques and materials yield 7 percent. Since many of the Asiatic commodities requisitioned as tax or coveted as trade items came in Canaanite containers, it is not surprising that 7 percent of the words refer to such containers (ceramic or basketry). International diplomacy accounts for 4 percent of the total, the cult 3 percent, and commerce 2 percent.[11]

It should be added that the most recent (and in many ways the most thorough) treatment of west-Semitic foreign words in Late Egyptian (that of James Hoch), in attempting to isolate the dialect of origin, most often is drawn to the coast rather than the hinterland of the Levant.[12]

A second type of Levantine sojourner in Egypt, especially common in the imperial period, was the prisoner of war or requisitioned laborer, shipped off to Egypt at Pharaoh's request. Although the Old and Middle Kingdoms were sensitive to manpower needs, which could only be met by forcibly transplanting foreigners to the banks of the Nile,[13] it was the empire of the New Kingdom that produced by far the largest number of captive or impressed Asiatics in Egypt. Firm control was exerted by the authorities over this alien population; each Asiatic was registered and put to work under Egyptian supervision, usually in the workhouse, in the weaving shop, or on the farms.[14] There is little evidence that communal groups were kept together in one part of the country, the whole purpose of the exercise being to meet the need for laborers all over

Egypt, and those who functioned as units, like the *apiru*[15] or the unspecified *Kharu*,[16] did so at construction sites and quarries and could be moved about. That they were momentarily quartered in one part of the country did not imply permanent domicile there. And nowhere during the New Kingdom is there any evidence that any part of this servile population attempted over time to retain its mores and preserve itself as a distinct ethnic entity.

A third type of sojourner, unlike the two groups mentioned above and not particularly welcomed by the Egyptians, was the Bedouin. From time immemorial, the waters of the Nile in both the delta and the valley have acted like a magnet on the wanderers of the Sinai with their promise of sustenance for man and beast in the dry season. (Interestingly, the bedu of Se'ir, according to Anastasi VI, make the trek in mid-June).[17] The donjons of the delta,[18] especially on the eastern side, were intended to control, if not block, their access to Lower Egypt, but even when the "Watch on the East," as it were, lapsed and blockhouses were abandoned, the bedu still did not come in great numbers, and their quest was mainly for the water holes. Such was the transhumant whom Merikare's father describes so eloquently, a description ending with the significant thumbnail judgment: "The Asiatic is a crocodile on the riverbank: He snatches on the lonely road, (but) he will never seize at the harbor of a populous city!"[19] Neferty betrays their main concern: The Wall of the Ruler, says he, will be built to keep them out "and the Asiatics shall not be allowed to come down to Egypt, that they might ask for water, beggar-fashion, to water their flocks."[20] We would err if for any period of Egypt's history we should imagine wandering nomads from western Asia constituting a significant element, or even a substantial minority, in the population of the delta west of the Bubastite branch. To find over 50 percent of the servants on one estate in the valley of the Nile with west-Semitic personal names[21] says nothing about the demography of the delta! For the same period (Dynasty XII-XIII), Canaanite personal names are occasionally found in the Memphite region, the Fayum, and the Thebaid,[22] but they are by no means numerous, and there is no evidence that these individuals belonged to a community composing a large percentage of the population of the delta.

The routes of access favored by the ingressing bedu clearly show their abhorrence of transit corridors that terminated in a maze of waterways. They route through the wady of LE 8, their umbilical cord, from the Km Wr;[23] and both LE 7 and 8, through their association with bedu, earned a reputation in the Middle Kingdom for isolation and encampments.[24] Further south, easy access to the Nile Valley was offered by the Wady Arabah (which accounts for Asiatic settlements near Atfih, toponyms like *Sharapa* and *'ayin* in the same region, and Asiatic personal names at El-Hibeh)[25] or Gebel Zeyt and a wady debouching into UE 16.[26]

The final type of sojourner is the occupier, a member of a large sedentary community that has taken up residence with or without the permission of the host country. In Egypt the best examples are the Meshwesh, Labu, and Mahaswen, and the extent of their settlement can be pinpointed with reasonable accuracy to the Fayum, the west delta, Behbit, and Pi-ese.[27]

But for our purposes, a more relevant case can be made of evidence from toponymy and orthography, and dating to the close of the fourth millennium B.C.E. In the earliest onomasticon of place names in the northeastern delta, among names that are later suppressed by secondary epithets, there exist unequivocal traces of name giving by non-Egyptian speakers using Semitic roots, which survived the turmoil of the Archaic period and became embedded, as it were, in the delta landscape. Similarly, in the nascent hieroglyphic script the language-specific nature of about a dozen signs points to their origin within a community familiar with, and in fact speaking, a Semitic language. Related to this name giving and script devising must be the introduction of various cultic motifs and symbols that partake of a Levantine, rather than a Nilotic, character: the divine herdsman and/or shepherd, the ram, the sea monster, the embattled mother and child and so forth. It has become fashionable in some anthropological circles to play down the effect of an external factor in the coming to birth of the pharaonic complex society in favor of a theory of autochthonous evolution. While this may be a salutary and chastening exercise, the evidence of recent excavations as well as toponomy and script strongly suggests that those parts of the delta lying closest to the frontier were host, in Late Predynastic times, to Semitic-speaking stock that enjoyed sufficient longevity and permanence to contribute markedly to the incipient culture of the state.[28]

From the XVIIIth through XXth Dynasty, one notes the total absence in LE 8, 13, or 14 of any evidence of a substantial resident population of Asiatics living in large measure unto itself. The documents of the time, both private and official, are not silent on the subject of the eastern delta, but they depict for us a tract combed by Medjay and desert patrols—designed specifically to keep aliens out—dotted with checkpoints and well-sited forts.[29] The eastern delta is, in fact, a sort of *limes* to be guarded by god, priest, and soldier; it is not a soft buffer zone, out of Egypt's effective control, inhabited by a foreign community speaking another language.

Of the types of sojourn reviewed above, it is clear that whoever wrote the narrative in Exodus is thinking of the last. The Israelites constitute a discrete community, largely serviced by their own people, living apart from the Egyptians in the land of Gšm,[30] on the eastern side of Lower Egypt,[31] even enjoying at times their own climate! The picture resembles that of a canton contiguous to Egypt rather than a dispersed ethnic labor force within the country.

The details of the picture, moreover, do not square with what we should expect of an Egyptian experience. The activity the Israelites are engaged in on behalf of the Egyptian state finds parallels in Asia, and the concept of "bondage organization" is not noticeably pharaonic.[32] The onomasticon upon which the Exodus account draws shows us an eastern delta of Saite, or early Persian, date seen through the skewed vision of an inhabitant of Judah.[33] The themes of the Sojourn and the Exodus, as embellished in the Pentateuch, belong in the realm of folklore to a large extent. They do not assist in any way in establishing the date or historicity of the Exodus or the true nature of the Sojourn.

ENDNOTES

[1] Whether or not the present Pentateuchal sequence (or any sequence, for that matter) for these three events is necessary must remain moot. But they do represent distinct motifs, found widely in literature and folklore outside the Bible. For the Miracle at the Sea, see P. Weimar, *Die Meerwunder erzählung* (Wiesbaden, 1985). For the drowning of a host (sometimes by the diversion of flowing water), cf. Herodotos ii.100; Strabo xvi.2.26; Diodorus i.30.3-7. "Wandering" was considered a contemptible characteristic of all bedu: cf. Merikare, in W. Helck, *Die Lehrefür König Merikare* (Wiesbaden, 1977), XXXIV; A.H. Gardiner, *Journal of Egyptian Archaeology* 39 (1953), p. 7; Gardiner and J. Černý, *Hieratic Ostraca* (Oxford, 1957), pl. 78;. Helck, *Vetus Testamentum* 18 (1968), pp. 472-480. On "conquests," see F.S. Frick, *The Formation of the State in Ancient Israel: A Survey of Models and Theories* (Sheffield, 1985); R.B. Coote and K.W. Whitelam, *The Emergence of Early Israel in Historical Perspective* (Sheffield, 1987); K.L. Younger, Jr., *Ancient Conquest Accounts: A Study in Ancient Near Eastern and Biblical Conquest Accounts* (Sheffield, 1990); V. Fritz, *Zeitschrift des deutschen Palästina-Vereins* 106 (1990), pp. 63-77.

[2] Berlin 8169; S. Sauneron and J. Yoyotte, *Revue d'égyptologie* 7 (1951), p. 69 n. 1; Helck, *Oriens Antiquus* 5 (1966), pp. 2f.

[3] Strabo xvii.1.18; A.B. Lloyd, *Herodotos Book II: A Commentary*, vol. 3 (Leiden, 1988), p. 224.

[4] R.A. Caminos, *The Chronicle of Prince Osorkon* (Rome, 1958), pp. 142, 144.

[5] Nitocris Stela 27; Caminos, *Journal of Egyptian Archaeology* 50 (1964), pp. 94f.

[6] G. Daressy, *Annales du Service des antiquitiés de l'Egypte* 18 (1918), p. 146.

[7] I.e., Naukratis: H. Gauthier, *Dictionnaire géographique* (Cairo, 1926), vol. 2, p. 87.

[8] On these garrisons see E. Bresciani, *"Le lettere aramaiche di Hermopoli,"* in *Atti Accademia Nazionale dei Liucei* (Rome, 1966), pp. 356-428, esp. 366f.; W. Kornfeld, *Wiener Zeitschrift für die Kunde Süd-und Ostasiens* 61 (1967), pp. 9-16; B. Porten and J.C. Greenfield, *Zeitschrift für die alttestamentliche Wissenschaft* 80 (1968), pp. 216-226; P. Grelot, *Chronique d'Égypte* 45 (1970), pp. 120ff.; K. van der Toorn, *Numen* 39:1 (1992), pp. 80-101. Individuals were salaried by the state: cf. A. Cowley, *Aramaic Papyri of the Fifth Century B.C.* (Oxford, 1923), no. 11.6; E.G Kraeling, *Aramaic Papyri in the Brooklyn Museum* (New Haven, 1953), no. 11.4; Padua Pap. I, vs. l. *Dgl* has been taken to mean "garrison": J.A. Fitzmyer, in *Near Eastern Studies in Honor of William Foxwell Albright*, ed. H. Goedicke (Baltimore, 1971), p, 148; cf. also J.B. Segal, *Aramaic Texts from North Saqqara* (London, 1983), nos. 19, 24, 62, et al.

[9] Degrees of acclimation are deceptively difficult to control. Far more significant and relevant for the historian are degrees of acceptance of and by an alien culture/community; but on this, archaeology, by nature, is not equipped to pass judgment. And a simple one-to-one interpretation of the archaeological record is sure to lead one astray. A priceless example of the futility of such an approach is the debate on the origins and identity of the Hyksos *solely* on the basis of the artifactual record of the excavations of Bietak, Holladay, and others: cf. M. Bietak, in A.F. Rainey, ed., *Egypt, Israel, Sinai* (Tel Aviv, 1987), pp. 41-56, and Bietak, *Bulletin of the American Schools of Oriental Research* 281 (1991), pp. 27-72 passim, esp. 32; R.S. Hallote, "Redefining the Hyksos," and C.A. Redmount, "Pottery and Ethnicity at Tell el-Maskhuta, Egypt" (both papers presented at the annual meeting of ASOR/SBL, Chicago, November 1994).

[10] J.J. Janssen, *Two Ancient Egyptian Ships' Logs* (Leiden, 1961), pp. 236-237.

[11] Cf. D.B. Redford, *Egypt, Canaan and Israel in Ancient Times* (Princeton, 1992), pp. 236-237.

[12] J.E. Hoch, *Semitic Words in Egyptian Texts of the New Kingdom and Third Intermediate Period* (Princeton, 1994).

[13] *Urkunden* I, 237.13-14, 240.3-4, 246.3; J. Lopez, *Las inscripciones rupestres faraonicas entre Korosko y Kasr Ibrim* (Madrid, 1966), nos. 27-28; Helck, *Studien zur Altägyptischen Kultur* 1 (1974), pp. 215ff.; Redford, *Scripta Mediterranea* 2 (1981), pp. 5-16, *Journal of the American Research Center in Egypt* 23 (1986), pp. 125-144, and *Egypt*, pp. 76-80. The text of Amenemhet II's inscription has appeared as H. Altenmüller, "Die Inschrift Amenemhets II aus dem Ptah-Tempel von Memphis," *Studien zur Altägyptischen Kultur* 18 (1991), pp. 1-48.

[14] Helck, *Die Beziehungen Aegyptens zur Vorderasien*, 2d ed. (Wiesbaden, 1972), pp. 342ff.; Redford, *Egypt*, pp. 221f.

[15] O. Loretz, *Habiru-Hebraeer* (Berlin/New York, 1984), pp. 35-44.

[16] Cf. P. Berlin 10620, rs. 9.

[17] Gardiner, *Late Egyptian Miscellanies* (Bruxelles, 1938), pp. 76-77; Caminos, *Late Egyptian Miscellanies* (Oxford, 1954), pp. 293-296.

[18] The terms vary over time, an indication of functional and lexical change. For "checkpoint" (*rthw*) and "fortress" (*mnnw*), see Gardiner, *Ancient Egyptian Onomastica* (Oxford, 1947), vol. 1, R 170A; H. Junker, *Gîza*, vol. 3 (Vienna, 1929), figs. 27-28; H.G. Fischer, *Dendera in the Third Millennium BC* (Locust Valley, 1968), p. 10 n. 47; W.M.F. Petrie, *Deshasheh* (London, 1896), pls. 3 and 6. For "keep, calabousse" (*hnrt*), see *Wörterbuch* III, 296.14-297.2; Neferty, P 33-34 (specifically of the eastern delta); W.C. Hayes, *A Papyrus of the Late Middle Kingdom in the Brooklyn Museum* (Brooklyn, 1956), pp. 37ff.; S. Quirke, *Revue d'égyptologie* 37 (1986), pp. 111 n. 24, 115 n. 37; inb/inbw (cf. *inb*, "to wall off" [J.M. Kruchten, *Le décret d'Horemheb* (Bruxelles, 1981), p. 148, line 3 (of the delta)]), cf. *inbw n hk³*,"the fort of the ruler," *Wörterbuch* I, 95.9; Neferty P 66-68; Sinuhe B 16-17; F. Gomaà, *Die Besiedlung Aegyptens während der mittleren Reiches* (Wiesbaden, 1987), vol. 1, pp. 129-130. For "fort, lock-up" (*htm*), cf. *Wörterbuch* III, 352.6-8; G.P.F. van den Boorn, *The Duties of the Vizier* (London, 1988), p. 44 ("enclosure covering all types of rooms, houses and spaces that ought to be locked"); applied to Sile on the northeastern frontier of the delta: Gardiner, *Onomastica*, vol. 2, pp. 202*ff.; Redford, *Egypt and Canaan in the New Kingdom* (Beersheva, 1990), pp. 29-30; Cairo 29306; Gauthier, *Dictionnaire géographique*, vol. 2, p. 121; W. Hayes, *Journal of Near Eastern Studies* 10 (1951), fig. 27 (DD, EE); M.A. Leahy, *Excavations at Malkata and the Birket Habu*, vol. 4, *The Inscriptions* (Warminster, 1975), p. 30, no. 14; K. Kitchen, ed., *Ramesside Inscriptions, Historical and Biographical*, 7 vols. (Oxford, 1968-), vol. 2, 12.12, 287.11, 288.7, 9, et al. For "fortress-tower" (*mktr = migdol*), Gauthier, *Dictionnaire géographique*, vol. 3, p. 2, 122. For "stronghold" (*nhtw*), *Wörterbuch* II, 317.11-12; D. Meeks, *Année lexicographique*, vol. 3 (Paris, 1982), p. 155; often the equivalent of "mercenary camp," P. Harris 76,8; 77,5 (where captured Libyan troops were quartered). In Saite

times and later the word "*sbty*," "fortified enclosure," came into use: P. Demotic Cairo 31169.i.9, iii.3.19; Daressy, *Annals du Service des antiquités de l'Egypte* 16 (1916), pp. 61f., and *Annals due Service des antiquites de l'Egypte* 18 (1918), p. 158. The term would seem to refer to large, rectilinear fortresses, like Tel Defenneh and Tel Kedwa on the eastern frontier, intended to house (foreign) troops: E. Oren, *Bulletin of the American Schools of Oriental Research* 256 (1984), pp. 7-44.

[19] Merikare, P 94-98.

[20] Neferty 66-68. On the *topos* of the Asiatic in Egyptian literature, see A. Loprieno, *Topos und Mimesis* (Wiesbaden, 1989).

[21] W. Hayes, *Papyrus*, pp. 87-109.

[22] Redford, *Egypt*, p. 78.

[23] F. Gomaà, *Aegyptens*, vol. 2, pp 131-132 (literature).

[24] Cf. P. Lacau and H. Chevrier, *Une Chapelle de Sesostris Ier a Karnak* (Cairo, 1969), pls. 41-42. *Hwwi* is not "stick" (Gomaà, *Aegyptens*, vol. 1, p. 126), but חחח, "camp". see Redford, "Some Observations on the Northern and North-eastern Delta in the Late Predynastic Period," in *Goedicke Festschrift* (Baltimore, 1994), n. 52.

[25] Caminos, *Chronicle*, pp. 142-44; Gardiner, *Papyrus Wilbour: Commentary* (Oxford, 1948), p. 49; W. Spiegelberg, *Zeitschrift für Ägyptische Sprache und Altertumskunde* 53 (1922), pp. 7-8.

[26] D. Kessler, *Studien zur Altägyptischen Kultur* 14 (1987), pp. 146-166.

[27] G. Maspero, *Memoire sur quelques Papyrus du Louvre* (Paris, 1875), no. 3169; Yoyotte, "Les principautés du Delta au temps de l'anarchie libyenne," in *Mélanges Maspero*, vol. 1, part 4 (Cairo, 1961), pp. 121-181; Leahy, ed., *Libya and Egypt c. 1300-750 BC* (London, 1990).

[28] See Redford, "North-eastern Delta," pp. 201-210.

[29] The road to Asia was firmly in Egyptian hands (cf. the itinerary at Karnak and in Anastasi I: Gardiner, *Journal of Egyptian Archaeology* 6 [1920], pp. 99-116; Oren, in Rainey, *Egypt, Israel, Sinai*, pp. 69-119), and Sile (Tel Hebwa: literature in J. Leclant, *Orientalia* 56 [1987], pp. 307-308, and 60 [1991], p. 177) effectually blocked any route attempting to negotiate the Pelusiac branch. Similarly, in the Wady Tumilat the fort at Tel er-Retabeh controlled access to the delta from the east with little difficulty: cf. Anastasi VI, 4,14-16. Other texts (cf. Anastasi V, 19,2-20,6; 25,2-27,3) attest to the efficiency of a system that controls both frontier and adjacent deserts through police and patrols. While there are pockets of Asiatic wine producers (Kitchen, *Ramesside Inscriptions*, vol. 7, p. 68, on the *Rekhty*-water northeast of Mendes) and bedu (Gardiner and Černý, *Hieratic Ostraca*, vol. 1, pl. 78), they are isolated and of little consequence.

[30] MT ארץ גשן is a distortion under the influence of Joshua 10:41 (with original locative *-ānu*) and the *bōsheth* vocalisation (J.M. Miller and J.H. Hayes, *A History of Ancient Israel and Judah* [Philadelphia, 1986], p. 139; L. Koehler and W. Baumgartner, *Hebräisches und aramäisches Lexikon zum Alten Testament* [Leiden, 1967], pp. 197-198). Whether or not *gōšen* derives from *gus*, a word for some kind of soil (so W.F. Albright, *Yahweh and the Gods of Canaan* [New York, 1968], p. 155 n. 8), must remain moot, but the word is clearly Semitic. The Gesef Arabias of the LXX is to be preferred, since it displays a superior knowledge of the geography of L.E. 20 and the Wady Tumilat: Helck, *Die Altaegyptische Gaue* (Wiesbaden, 1974), pp. 197-198. A derivation from *gśm*, "rain, heavy showers" (C. Gordon, *Ugaritic Textbook* [Rome, 1965], no. 626; A. Murtonen, *Hebrew in its West-semitic Setting* [Leiden, 1989], vol. 1, sec. BB, p. 142), is most unlikely in view of the context. Almost certainly, ארץ גשן reflects the name *Gashmu*, the Qedarite chieftain who controlled the tract in the early fifth century B.C.E.:

W.J. Dumbrell, *Bulletin of the American Schools of Oriental Research* 203 (1971), pp. 42-43; A. Lemaire, *Revue biblique* 81 (1974), pp. 63ff.; F.M. Cross, *Catholic Biblical Quarterly* 48 (1986), pp. 387-394.

[31] Goshen is usually located along the Saft el-Henne–Faqus–Wady Tumilat arc (literature in B. Halpern, in *Eretz-Israel* 24, ed. S. Ahituv and B.A. Levine [1993], pp. 94*-96*, nn. 10, 27), but the uncritical acceptance of the antiquity of the name must occasion embarrassment: It has not yet appeared in early hieroglyphic texts! The alleged occurrence in P. Kahun I, 14, of Middle Kingdom date (Gomaà, *Aegyptens*, vol. 2, p. 127) has been misread and should be rendered "lo! he (the king) is the rampart of a wall of metal of *Sšm*-land," where the latter is to be linked to the word *sšmt* (cf. *Wörterbuch* IV, 538.12) and derived from the word for "malachite" (J.M. Harris, *Lexicographical Studies in Ancient Egyptian Minerals* [Berlin, 1961], p. 132). While the Piankhy Stela (N.-C. Grimal, *La stèle triomphale de Pi[ankhy]...* [Cairo, 1981]) and the Wady el-Arish naos (G. Goyon, *Kêmi* 6 [1936], pp. 1ff.), both of which bear upon the toponymy of the region, do not mention anything resembling a "Goshen," the Saft el-henne naos (E. Naville, *The Shrine of Saft el-Henneh and the Land of Goshen* [London, 1888], pl. 6.2-3) twice refers to a place or district which has been read *Qs*(?): "[The per]fect [god (i.e., Nektanebo I, author of the naos)], Lord of the Two Lands who made this (the naos) of his own volition in order to make the god comfortable in his shrine, after H.M. came to *Qs*(?), propitiating this august god Sopdu, Lord of the East (principal deity of Saft el-Henne) ... H.M. himself gave directions to construct these cult-images of the gods of *Qs*(?) upon this naos J" Since the deities in question are those of Pi-Sopdu, *Qs*(?) would appear to refer to Saft el-Henne. One cannot avoid, therefore, citing the late Ptolemaic geographical list (*Edfu* VI, 42, no. 71) in which a *Qsm*(?) is mentioned as the main city of the Pi-Sopdu township (=L.E. 20: Helck, *Die Altaegyptische Gaue*, p. 198). From the apocopated form (?), *Qs*(?), runs the argument, derives the toponym fakoussa, mod. Faqus (Strabo xvii.1.26). But there remains the possibility that *Qsm* is an erroneous reading. The implication of Genesis 46:32-34 and 47:1-6, that Goshen was ideally suited for herdsmen, would seem to point to the Wady Tumilat around Tel el-Maskhuta (an access route for bedu): R. North, *Archaeobiblical Egypt* (Rome, 1967), pp. 80-86; J. Simons, *The Geographical and Topographical Texts of the Old Testament* (Leiden, 1959), pp. 244ff.; C. Westermann, *Genesis Kapital 37-50* (Neukirchen, 1982), p. 161; W. H. Schmidt, *Exodus, Sinai, Mose* (Darmstadt, 1983), p. 27; H. Donner, *Geschichte des Volkes Israel* (Gottingen, 1984), p. 89.

[32] Brick making and the construction of cities were precisely the activities assigned by the Assyrians to their P.O.W.s in bondage: J.V. Kinnier-Wilson, *The Nimrud Wine-lists* (Hertford, 1972), p. 92; B. Oded, *Mass Deportation and Deportees in the Neo-Assyrian Empire* (Wiesbaden, 1979), pp. 60, 67.

[33] Redford, in Rainey, *Egypt, Israel, Sinai*, pp. 137-161; and *Egypt*, pp. 408-422.

4

IS THERE ANY ARCHAEOLOGICAL EVIDENCE FOR THE EXODUS?

William G. Dever

B efore the modern era, the historicity of the Exodus was taken for granted. By the late 19th century, however, the rise of higher, or literary, criticism had called the biblical account into question. Among the initial reactions of Evangelicals and conservative biblical scholars to this blow at the heart of biblical faith was to invoke the then-new "science of archaeology" (as it was often called) to demonstrate the historicity of the Exodus-Conquest narratives by producing extra-biblical "proofs," textual or artifactual.

Until about a decade ago, this attempt at archaeological confirmation was still being pursued. Today, however, all that has changed, as I shall show. And with new models of indigenous Canaanite origins for early Israel, there is neither place nor need for an exodus from Egypt.[1] Let us examine both the traditional and the newer data to see where we now stand.

POSING THE PROBLEM: THE LITERARY AND HISTORICAL ISSUES

A. THE BIBLICAL NARRATIVES

The biblical narratives take the Exodus story from the descent of the patriarchs into Egypt through the enslavement and ultimate liberation of the Hebrews and, finally, to the crossing of the Sinai and Negev deserts into Transjordan opposite Jericho. As is well known, this story, running through much of the Pentateuch, contains a number of Egyptian elements. The Joseph story has rather close parallels in Egyptian Wisdom and other literature, such as the Tale of Two Brothers.[2] The name Moses contains the same element as such Egyptian names as Ramesses. A few other biblical names are transparently Egyptian: Hophni, Phinehas, and the midwives of the Hebrew slaves, Shiphrah and Puah. The Hebrew slave camps are located rather precisely in the eastern delta, specifically, at Pithom and Ramesses, XIXth Dynasty sites that are actually known (Exodus 1:11; see below). These would all seem to be authentic traces of an original Egyptian *Sitz im Leben* for the biblical narratives.

B. THE QUESTION OF HISTORICAL CONTEXT

There are, however, many problems with such a simplistic analysis of the text. For instance, the scant references above are the only real Egyptian touches in the entire biblical narrative. One is struck by the glaring omissions of other specific references, in a supposedly historical account, among them the absence of the name of the Egyptian king (in this case, Ramesses II), who is simply called Pharaoh. Should the biblical writers not have known and included the name of such a pivotal actor in the drama?

A further problem in the text concerns chronology. In 1 Kings 6:1, which relates the dedication of Solomon's temple in Jerusalem, it is said that this event occurred 480 years after the Exodus, in the fourth year of Solomon's reign. Since Solomon's accession date of c. 960 B.C.E. can be calculated via synchronisms with astronomically fixed Assyrian and Babylonian king lists, we would place the date of the Exodus at c. 1440 B.C.E. (supported then by other schemes of chronological reckoning in the biblical materials). Yet the overwhelming archaeological and extra-biblical textual data place the immediate background of the Israel settlement in Canaan in the mid to late 13th century B.C.E., two centuries later. Despite the attempts of a few fundamentalists like John Bimson and Bryant Wood to defend the Bible by adducing archaeological evidence to place the biblical Exodus and Conquest accounts in the 15th century B.C.E., the vast majority of archaeologists and historians (and even most biblical scholars) have given up such desperate and futile attempts to date the settlement to the 15th century B.C.E.[3]

The related attempt to see in the Asiatic Hyksos the biblical patriarchs, and to connect the account of the Exodus and Conquest with the XVIIIth Dynasty expulsion of the Hyksos and with the destruction of the Middle Bronze Age sites in Palestine in the early 15th century B.C.E., goes back, of course, to the Jewish historian Josephus. And it seems to make sense of the biblical texts, when read simply at face value. The problem is that all such reconstructions as the above are now rendered absolutely impossible by the accumulating archaeological evidence, as we shall see.

Despite obvious difficulties, many biblical scholars, such as Nahum Sarna, continue to rationalize the problems with the biblical texts, which seems to me simply either wishful thinking or special pleading.[4] If we stand back, however, and look dispassionately at the entire Descent-Exodus-Wilderness-Conquest cycle in the Hebrew Bible, it reads much better as folktale—i.e., as myth, rather than history. The problem then shifts: It becomes one of literary and, finally, theological critique. That is, how and why and when did the literary tradition of the Exodus in the

Hebrew Bible develop, and become so dominant in Israelite faith and history, if it did not rest on historical memory? To that we shall return briefly at the end.

THE ARCHAEOLOGICAL EVIDENCE: NEW DATA AND NEW MODELS

L et us turn now to the archaeological evidence, which for many holds out the promise of recovering the actual historical background of the emergence of Israel in Canaan and, in my opinion, can now do just that. Here we cannot simply look at the Exodus in isolation but must regard any such event as an integral part of the entire settlement process and the biblical tradition that grew up around it.

A. POSSIBLE EGYPTIAN CONTEXTS

I t is well known that nowhere in Egyptian literature, in history, or in the archaeological record is there a reference or artifact that would indicate that the "proto-Israelites" were ever in Egypt. We confront virtual silence on the Egyptian side. The one text we do have, the famous Victory Stele of Merneptah, c. 1207 B.C.E., recognizes a people (sic) denoted "Israel," not in Egypt but rather in Canaan, and the text evidently knows nothing else about them. How could that be if these newly established "Israelites" in Canaan were former Hebrew slaves, recently escaped from Pharaoh and his armies in the eastern delta?[5]

Among the scant references in the Hebrew Bible to specific details of an Egyptian sojourn that might be identified archaeologically is the reference to the Israelites being in servitude in the delta cities of Pithom and Ramesses (Exodus 1:11). Pithom (Per-Atum) can possibly be identified with Tell el-Maskhuta, or with nearby Tell el-Retabe,[6] and Ramesses (Pi-Ramesse) has now almost certainly been located at Tell el-Dabʿa, near Qantir, by the recent excavations of Manfred Bietak. All three are among the few delta sites known from recent excavations to have been Asiatic (i.e., Canaanite) colonies in Egypt in the Middle Kingdom/Hyksos era (Dynasties XII-XVII, c. 1991-1530 B.C.E.). Tell el-Dabʿa was, in fact, the Hyksos capital of Avaris, destroyed c. 1530 B.C.E. with the expulsion of the Hyksos at the beginning of the XVIIIth Dynasty. Now two of these sites also have Ramesside levels of the 13th or 12th century B.C.E. Thus Tell el-Dabʿa, although deserted throughout the New Kingdom after its destruction, was reoccupied in the time of Ramesses II (Stratum B), in the early to mid-13th century B.C.E. (Ramesses II = 1304-1237 B.C.E).[7] Similarly, Tell el-Maskhuta has no occupation after the Middle Kingdom/Hyksos levels until the Saite horizon (late seventh century B.C.E).[8] Tell el-Retabe was also occupied in the Middle Kingdom, abandoned in the New Kingdom, then reoccupied in the XIXth Dynasty and onward (c. 1200 B.C.E. on).[9]

Is it merely fortuitous that these delta sites, some known to the biblical writers, had a substantial Canaanite or Asiatic presence in the so-called patriarchal period, and that the two were rebuilt under Egyptian aegis in Ramesside times, which is when an Israelite sojourn in Egypt would have to be placed archaeologically? The new evidence is not conclusive, of course (i.e., there are questions regarding the exact location and date of "Pithom"), but it may lend support to the long-held view of some biblical scholars that at least some constituent elements of later Israel had actually stemmed from Egypt, such as the "House of Joseph" (below). Only one thing is certain, however, and that is that the scant Egyptian historical evidence points unanimously to a 13th-century B.C.E. (not 15th) date, if any, for an Israelite exodus.[10]

Moving on to the Sinai tradition, the crossing of the Red (Reed) Sea is obviously a miraculous tale that can in no way be validated or even illuminated by archaeological investigation. Furthermore, of the subsequent wandering in the wilderness theme (Numbers 33:1-49), little can be said archaeologically. If indeed the Israelites are to be pictured as a band of wanderers, or even as semi-sedentary pastoralists, we would still probably find no remains of their ephemeral camps in the desert.[11] Thus all attempts to trace the route of the Sinai crossing, as wishfully portrayed on maps in biblical atlases, have been doomed to failure, reduced to inconclusive efforts to identify hazy topographical references in the Bible with modern Arab place names that usually have no clear historical associations. Emmanuel Anati has recently claimed that he has located biblical Mt. Sinai at Har Karkom, in the western Negev; but few will find the petroglyphs and other data convincing evidence that this is anything more than another of the holy mountains frequented from time immemorial by nomads of the desert.[12]

The only second-millennium B.C.E. Sinai route that is attested archaeologically is the northern route along the coastal dunes—the "Way of Horus"—which archaeological investigation has indeed illuminated, precisely in Egyptian New Kingdom times.[13] But this is the route that was bypassed, according to the biblical tradition, because of Egyptian control. All we can say is that recent, extensive exploration of the entire Sinai by Israeli archaeologists, geologists, and others has turned up no Middle or Late Bronze Age presence in the central or southern Sinai whatsoever. Thus our current, detailed knowledge of this remote and hostile area calls into question the biblical tradition of some two million people wandering there (Numbers 11:21) for some 40 years (Deuteronomy 2:7). The barren terrain and sparse oases might have supported a few straggling nomads, but no more than that.

The description of a 38-year encampment at Kadesh-Barnea, which is prominent in the biblical tradition, has long intrigued biblical scholars and archaeologists. Following the topographical indications in the Bible, Kadesh-Barnea has been quite plausibly identified since the 19th century with the well-known oasis at ʿAin el-Qudeirat, near Quseima on the modern Israel-Egypt border. The small tell near the spring was found in 1956 by Moshe Dothan[14] and was then extensively excavated to virgin

Nelson Glueck. *An American rabbi, Glueck epitomized an earlier era's romantic notion of biblical archaeology. Whether dashing across desert sands in a jeep or trudging on foot, Glueck did important work surveying sights in Transjordan and the Sinai. Despite his desire to corroborate the biblical tradition, Glueck's site surveys indicated that ancient Edom, Moab, and Ammon were sparsely populated and defended at the beginning of the Iron Age—when, if the biblical account were accurate, the Israelites would have been cutting a victorious swath through them on the way to conquering the Promised Land.*

soil in 1976-1982 by Rudolph Cohen.[15] The latter has shown conclusively that the remains consist of three successive Israelite forts (Levels I-III) of the tenth to seventh/sixth centuries B.C.E., with no evidence of earlier occupation, not even scattered sherds. Thus the present evidence for the Kadesh-Barnea episode has little historical basis; it appears to have become significant only in the time of the United Monarchy, when the Exodus theme was crystallizing in the literary tradition and when a pilgrimage festival to the site apparently began.

We turn now to Transjordan. The first phase of the conquest of Canaan, according to the biblical accounts, focused on central and southern Transjordan, which the tribes of Gad, Reuben, and half-Manasseh are said to have occupied. The incoming Israelites are portrayed as encountering a settled population in Ammon, Moab, and Edom. Among specific cities mentioned as taken (and by implication destroyed) are Heshbon and Dibon, obviously to be identified with the large tells of Hesbân and Dhibân, respectively. Yet extensive excavations of both have revealed that neither site has any Late Bronze occupation, as the biblical tradition of the Exodus would require. Hesbân has scant 12th- to 11th-century material, with Iron Age occupation beginning principally in the 10th century B.C.E.[16] Dhibân may have some Iron I material, but nothing earlier; and most of the Iron Age remains are eighth to seventh century B.C.E.[17] Thus neither site can have been destroyed by the Israelites under Joshua in the mid-13th century B.C.E., as posited by Numbers 21:21-30. The same is true of Madeba, which has produced thus far only a 12th-century B.C.E. tomb for this horizon.[18]

Elsewhere in Transjordan, the general picture of Late Bronze and early Iron I occupation is complex, but it is clear that there is relatively little sedentary occupation of southern Transjordan in the Late Bronze Age. Nelson Glueck's surveys in the 1930s and 1940s already suggested this (although he interpreted the evidence as supporting the biblical tradition of early Israelite settlement, i.e., as providing an early 12th-century B.C.E. context). Subsequent correction and expansion of Glueck's site maps, including the discovery of a few more Late Bronze sites farther north in the Jordan Valley and upon the plateau, has not, in my opinion, substantially changed the picture. Newer excavated evidence from Amman, the Beqaʿ Valley, Sahab, Irbid, Tell es-Saʿidiyeh, Deir ʿAllā, Kataret es-Samra, and a few other sites, as well as surveys from northern Jordan, the Jordan Valley, and Edom, all yield the same picture. Moab and Edom were not yet established, fortified kingdoms that would have posed any threat to Israelite tribes moving through the area in the late 13th or early 12th century B.C.E., and even Ammon was rather sparsely occupied and defended.[19] Thus, throughout most of southern Transjordan in Late Bronze to Iron I, apart from a few settled towns, pastoralists and nomads must have dominated the countryside, like the Shasu tribes well known from Egyptian New Kingdom texts.[20] In Moab, Heshbon and Dibon did not become significant urban centers until the ninth to eighth centuries B.C.E.[21] The majority of the Iron Age sites known in Edom through excavation began only in the eighth or seventh century B.C.E., such as ʿArôʿer, Buseirah (Bozrah), Tawilan, and Umm el-Biyarah.[22] Thus the notion of large-scale 13th- to 12th-century B.C.E. Israelite military campaigns in southern Transjordan, or even of peaceful settlement there, is no longer tenable. The occupational history of the region simply does not fit. As for destructions, the only known Late Bronze Age II destructions are farther north—at Deir ʿAllā, Tell es-Saʿidiyeh, and Irbid—in Gilead; and in all cases, both the biblical identification and the agents of destruction remain unclear.

While archaeologists are unanimous on the lack of a Late Bronze Age Transjordanian context for Israelite origins, a few biblical scholars have persisted. Robert Boling's small monograph on Transjordan[23] attempts to use the scant archaeological survey data on a few late Late Bronze Age sites to provide an actual historical context for the Exodus tradition. However, forced or even unwarranted archaeological conclusions and irrelevant theological presuppositions render this work largely useless. Virtually its only value is to distinguish earlier Israel (my proto-Israelites) from early Israel. But the data surveyed here show that there is simply no archaeological evidence that Boling's earliest Israel was ever in Transjordan.[24] Finally, the Israeli archaeologist Adam Zertal has tried to revive the old Alt-Noth hypothesis that the early Israelites were pastoral nomads from Transjordan, gradually moving across the Jordan in the process of becoming sedentarized.[25] But if there is little Late Bronze Age context for urban sites in Transjordan, there is none whatsoever for pastoral nomads. In my view, these attempts to provide archaeological justification for the nomadic ideal in ancient Israel are simply nostalgia for a biblical past that never was.[26]

William Foxwell Albright. *The doyen of biblical archaeologists, Albright dominated the field during the middle years of this century. He and his followers hoped to uncover evidence of the conquest of Canaan as recorded in the Book of Joshua. Sites such as Jericho and Ai, however, have not yielded such evidence. Today most scholars believe that the Israelites either infiltrated Canaan peacefully from outside and/or emerged from within Canaanite society.*

Finally, we need to look at the supposed conquest of western Palestine. The biblical tradition dealing with the main phase of the occupation of the land of Canaan west of the Jordan is too well known to need summarizing here (compare the principal accounts in Joshua, plus Numbers 21:1-3 and Judges 1). Since the infancy of modern topographical and archaeological research more than a century ago, biblical scholars and archaeologists have sought to locate the numerous cities said to have been taken and to identify 13th- to 12th-century B.C.E. destruction layers that might be attributed to incoming Israelites. Indeed, confirming the Israelite conquest of Canaan archaeologically became one of the major priorities on the agenda of the "biblical archaeology" movement led by Albright and his followers from c. 1925 to 1970, adopting almost exclusively the conquest model of Joshua.[27] This approach was also taken up by several prominent members of the Israeli school, notably Yigael Yadin.[28] And the effort still continues among a few conservative biblical scholars, most of whom, however, are forced to opt for the now totally discredited 15th-century date for the Exodus.[29]

While the conquest model derived, of course, from the Book of Joshua long held sway in both biblical and archaeological circles, it has had to be abandoned in light of much newer data from archaeological surveys and excavations, mostly of the past decade. Peaceful infiltration, peasant revolt, and symbiosis models now dominate the field, as will be seen from even a glance at the most authoritative recent synthesis, Israel Finkelstein's *Archaeology of the Israelite Settlement*.[30]

It is now abundantly clear that the destructions claimed at numerous late-13th- to early-12th-century B.C.E. sites—Jericho, ʿAi, and others—disappear upon closer examination. Only Hazor XIII, and perhaps Late Bronze Age Bethel, could possibly be attributed to incoming Israelites, and even these are doubtful. More recently, the destruction of the lower city at Hazor (Stratum XIII), while undoubtedly dramatic, has been dated earlier than the estimate of c. 1225 B.C.E. by Yadin,[31] who saw it as the work of the Israelites. If it is moved as early as 1250 B.C.E., it is less likely to have been connected with the Israelite settlement, which falls principally in the early 12th century B.C.E. The suggestion that Late Bronze Age Bethel was destroyed by incoming Israelites was originally Albright's and depends solely upon the witness of the biblical text, which is somewhat suspect.

Two Late Bronze Age sites that were not destroyed but may have been settled by the early Israelites should be noted here. Tel Dan VII (Canaanite Laish) generally shows little or no destruction, and it may simply have been taken over peacefully by Israelites sometime in the 12th century B.C.E.[32] The same is true of Canaanite Shechem (Stratum XII), which shows marked continuity of the Late Bronze Age *migdal* temple in Field V, a fact that accords well with the biblical tradition that

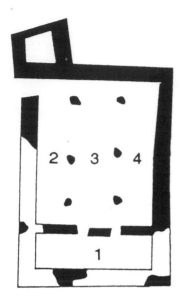

A Four-Room House. *Together with collar-rim jars, this type of architecture is characteristic of Israelite culture, although examples have also been found elsewhere. In its simplest form (drawing at left), a four-room house was composed of one long narrow room (1, at bottom) with three rooms, separated by pillars, jutting from it. In practice, the rooms were often subdivided and additional rooms added along the periphery (see photo opposite). Of the three rooms, the middle one (3) was probably uncovered, serving as a courtyard and containing an oven. The inhabitants lived and slept on a second level, with the ground floor given over for animals.* Drawing courtesy Israel Finkelstein, Archaeology of the Israelite Settlement, Israel Exploration Society.

Shechem came into the Israelite confederation through treaty, not by conquest.[33]

It now seems that the 12th-century B.C.E. proto-Israelites (as I would prefer to call them) were largely indigenous peoples of Palestine, perhaps displaced Canaanites, opening up and settling the hill country frontiers. The dozens of early Iron I hill-country villages—which we now know to be associated with a sweeping shift in settlement type and pattern and with relatively sudden demographic changes—are located precisely in those areas that were not heavily occupied in the 14th to 13th century B.C.E. or dominated by Late Bronze Age Canaanite city-states. These villages are found principally in the central hill country, but they are also found to some extent in Lower Galilee and the northern Negev. Almost without exception, these Iron I villages are small, unwalled sites, established *de novo* in the early 12th century B.C.E. Then after several phases of occupation these villages were abandoned in the late 11th to early 10th century B.C.E. as renewed urbanism began to develop and the nascent Israelite state moved toward the founding of the United Monarchy.[34]

I believe that we can tentatively connect these Iron I villages with the

emergence of an ethnic group that is characterized by later biblical and extra-biblical textual sources (the Merneptah Stele) as Israelites. The best known of these villages are those excavated at ʿAi, Radannah, Giloh, and ʿIzbet Sartah in the hill country and probably at Tel Masos in the northern Negev. Altogether, however, at least 300 such sites are known through recent surface surveys.[35]

The typical distinguishing features of these villages are their location on hilltops near arable lands, especially in areas where the hillsides are suitable for terracing; a distinctive type of four-room courtyard house that is well adapted to extended family groupings, animal husbandry, and the storage of agricultural surpluses; the widespread use of cisterns and silos near domestic installations; and (perhaps) the introduction of new implements of iron. The early Iron I pottery of these village sites is overwhelmingly in the Late Bronze Age Canaanite tradition, except for a few features: (1) the absence of Late Mycenaean and Late Cypriot imports (including Late Mycenaean IIIC, Late Bronze Age, and its local Philistine monochrome and bichrome offshoots); (2) the occurrence at most sites of distinctive large collar-rim store jars, which, although derived from Late Bronze Age-style pithoi and occasionally attested at Iron I non-Israelite sites, may still serve as a useful type fossil for the hill-country villages under consideration.[36]

The economy, social structure, and political order of these Iron I proto-Israelite villages would seem to reflect a predominantly agrarian movement accompanied by a strong egalitarian thrust. Lawrence Stager[37] has analyzed both individual house forms and village layout, suggesting that they reflect almost precisely the socioeconomic structure of early Israel as reconstructed from numerous passages in Joshua, Judges, and Samuel. The large courtyard house is equivalent to the nuclear family with which an individual (Hebrew *gever*) identifies. The cluster of two to three houses in a typical multi-house compound reflects the extended, multigenerational family (Hebrew *bêt ʾāb*, house of the father). The several dozen such compounds in the whole village then suggest a large kinship group, like current stem families in the Middle East (Hebrew *mišpāḥāh*, clan). At all levels, however, one is struck by the lack of any evidence for elites in the Iron I villages.

The driving force behind the Israelite ethnic movement may indeed have been Yahwism, as the later biblical sources maintain, or the revolutionary social reforms of a peasant revolt, as Norman K. Gottwald and many other biblical scholars have argued. But however clearly the social and economic changes accompanying this ethnic movement may be seen in material culture remains, I would suggest that the ideology of our proto-Israelites will be reflected only indirectly in the archaeological record. Some, of course, would question whether we can even identify the archaeological assemblage as Israelite, but I am not so skeptical.[38] In any case, all we can say thus far is that between the late 13th century B.C.E. and sometime in the mid-11th century B.C.E., there occurred such far-reaching socioeconomic, technological, and cultural changes in central Palestine that the millennia-old Bronze Age may be said to have given way to a new order, the Iron Age, dominated soon by the emergent Israelite state. Yet all of these developments appear to be part of indigenous sociocultural changes at the end of the Late Bronze Age and the beginning of the Iron Age. They are natural and even predictable oscillations in the long settlement history of Palestine, not unique episodes that the archaeologist or historian is forced to explain by positing marauding hordes from the desert, wholesale destructions, and abrupt changes in material culture (much less divine intervention).[39]

The implication of the new picture of indigenous Late Bronze Age Canaanite origins for the majority of the early Israelite population is clear. Not only is there no archaeological evidence for an exodus, there is no need to posit such an event. We can account for Israelite origins, historically and archaeologically, without presuming any Egyptian background. As a Syro-Palestinian archaeologist, I regard the historicity of the Exodus as a dead issue, despite this symposium's raising it again.

There are, no doubt, theological problems that this negative evidence presents, but I leave such problems to others. I would only observe in passing that if one regards the biblical accounts as story rather than history (i.e., as literature), amenable to literary analysis, then the task of critical scholarship perhaps becomes more manageable.[40] That is, one need not pose the question of historicity but simply of the formation and transmission of a literary tradition. In this case, it is principally the Joshua tradition—one of mass migration and external military conflict—that we must confront, since the alternate account in Judges presupposes no such conquest. Indeed, it offers a realistic portrait of sedentarization and gradual assimilation of the Israelites over a period of as long as two centuries.

If one asks why the Israelite historiographers preserved two diametrically opposed versions of their own history, we can at least offer new critical approaches that may prove constructive. Recent structuralist analyses, such as those of Polzin,[41] Gottwald, and others, have suggested that the redactors of the later, dominant Deuteronomic tradition were fully aware of the radically divergent nature of the Joshua and Judges materials they incorporated, but they left them in tension in a deliberately dialectic manner. As Gottwald puts it, "By counterposing speech about how the Canaanites *must be* and *were* destroyed, against speech about how Canaanites *remained* in the land and were even *accepted* into Israel, DH (the Deuteronomic Historian) weaves an ironic exposition on the problematic of carrying out God's commands."[42]

The fact is that most ancient peoples contrived origin myths for themselves that were later incorporated into national epics, despite their sometimes fantastical character, as did the Greeks and others. In the case of the Israelite historiographers, it is possible that oral tradition had preserved the memory of Canaanite groups in Egypt during the Hyksos period and their subsequent expulsion. If that were the case, it would have been easy to connect these events, as well as others down into the XIXth Dynasty, with the prehistory of Israel. And as Baruch Halpern has suggested, the tenth century B.C.E.—when the literary traditions of the J and E narratives of the Pentateuch were crystallizing—would have provided an ideal *Sitz im Leben* for incorporating Egyptian motifs into the Hebrew national epic. On the other hand, Redford[43] has argued persuasively that all the Egyptian motifs in the biblical accounts of the Exodus would fit best in the Saite, or Persian, period (c. fifth century B.C.E.) and perhaps only then. In that case, the entire Exodus tradition would have to be assigned to the P (or Priestly) source of redactors, who shaped the final version of the Pentateuch precisely in the Persian period.[44]

Finally, of the Joshua tradition, however folkloristic it may be, it must nevertheless be acknowledged that these materials may contain some raw-source data for the historian. We should observe that the evidence does not rule out the possibility that some constituents of the later Israelite tribal confederation may have derived from Egypt. In this connection, it is worth remembering that many biblical scholars have long held that only the House of Joseph, or elements of the later tribes of Benjamin and Judah, which have disproportionately shaped the later literary tradition in the Hebrew Bible, were ever in Egypt. The fact that most of the numerous Iron I or proto-Israelite villages we now have are in the area of the Benjamin-Judah tribal territories may lend credence to that suggestion. However, even if this area is the chief locus of early Israelite occupation, there is no direct archaeological evidence of Egyptian origins for the settlers, as we have seen, so the question must remain open.

CONCLUSION

A ncient Israel's problem in comprehending her own history was the same as ours. How to account for the unique reality of the people of Israel? The biblical writers fell back on the only analogy they had, historical experience, which for them was their own firsthand knowledge of the power of Yahweh over their pagan neighbors and his ability to save and shape them as his people—despite their obscure origins, their lack of merit, and their disobedience. In the end, the biblical writers concluded that Israel's election was nothing less than a miracle, and who are we, their spiritual heirs, to disagree? It is, as this symposium has shown, at least a mystery. To put it another way, the biblical study of the Exodus is not so much history as it is *haggadah*.

ENDNOTES

[1] The literature on "Israelite origins" is rapidly proliferating, but for orientation and references see I. Finkelstein, *The Archaeology of the Israelite Settlement* (Jerusalem: Israel Exploration Society, 1988); R.B. Coote, *Early Israel: A New Horizon* (Minneapolis: Fortress Press, 1990); N.K. Gottwald, "Recent Studies of the Social World of Premonarchic Israel,"

in *Currents in Research: Biblical Studies*, vol. 1 (1993), pp. 163-189; Finkelstein and N. Na'aman, *From Nomadism to Monarchy: Archaeological and Historical Aspects of Early Israel* (Jerusalem: Israel Exploration Society, 1994); W.G. Dever, "Ceramics, Ethnicity, and the Question of Israel's Origins," *Biblical Archaeologist* 58:4 (1995), pp. 200-213.

[2] See D.B. Redford, *A Study of the Biblical Story of Joseph (Genesis 37-50)*, Vetus Testamentum Supplements (Leiden: Brill, 1970), and his chapter in this volume; D. Irvin, "The Joseph and Moses Stories as Narrative in the Light of Ancient Near Eastern Narrative," in J.H. Hayes and J.M. Miller, eds., *Israelite and Judean History* (Philadelphia: Westminster Press, 1977), pp. 180-212; cf. Coote and D.R. Ord, *The Bible's First History: From Eden to the Court of David with the Yahwist* (Philadelphia: Fortress Press, 1989), pp. 146-166.

[3] The latest, and most bizarre, reworking of chronology is that of P. James et al., *Centuries of Darkness: A Challenge to the Conventional Chronology of Old World Archaeology* (London: Jonathan Cape, 1991); but cf. the devastating critiques (including my own) in A. Leonard, Jr., ed., *A Review of Peter James et al.*, Colloquenda Mediterranea (London: Loid Publishing, 1993). For the old "high date" of the Exodus, see J. Bimson, *Redating the Exodus and Conquest*, rev. ed. (Sheffield: Almond Press, 1986); B. Wood, "Did the Israelites Conquer Jericho? A New Look at the Archaeological Evidence," *Biblical Archaeology Review* 16:2 (1990), pp. 44-57.

[4] N. Sarna, "Israel in Egypt: The Egyptian Sojourn and the Exodus," in *Ancient Israel: A Short History from Abraham to the Destruction of the Temple*, ed. H. Shanks (Washington, DC: Biblical Archaeology Society, 1988), pp. 31-52; see also S. Herrmann, *Israel in Egypt* (London: SCM Press, 1973).

[5] On the Merneptah Stele, see M. Hasel, " 'Israel' in the Merneptah Stele," *Bulletin of the American Schools of Oriental Research* 290 (1994), pp. 45-61.
    Frank Yurco has attempted to show that the well-known Karnak temple inscriptions attributed to Ramesses III (1198-1166 B.C.E.) actually belong to Merneptah (1212-1202 B.C.E.) and, further, that among the peoples portrayed in the "victory scene" (i.e., from Merneptah's campaign, c. 1207 B.C.E.) are portraits of our proto-Israelites. See further Yurco's chapter in this volume, and cf. Redford, also in this volume.

[6] See J.H. Holladay, Jr., *Tell el-Maskhuta: Preliminary Report of the Wadi Tumilat Project, 1978-1979* (Malibu: Undena Publications, 1982), pp. 3-6.

[7] On Tell el-Dabᶜa, see M. Bietak, *Avaris and Piramesse: Archaeological Exploration in the Eastern Nile Delta*, rev. ed. (1986; reprint, *Proceedings of the British Academy* 65 [1979]), pp. 225-296. For a revision of Bietak's chronology, however, see Dever, "Tell el-Dabᶜa and Levantine Middle Bronze Age Chronology," *Bulletin of the American Schools of Oriental Research* 284 (1991), pp. 73-79 and references there.

[8] Holladay, *Tell el-Maskhuta*, p. 4 n. 6

[9] Holladay, *Tell el-Maskhuta*, pp. 3-6.

[10] Note that we refer here only to the historical *Sitz im Leben*. Below I shall stress that the biblical/textual setting seems to require a much later date, in the Persian period; cf. Redford, in this volume. On the biblical narratives and their historical presuppositions, see further Herrmann, *Israel in Egypt*, pp. 19-50; Miller "The Israelite Occupation of Canaan," in Hayes and Miller, *Israelite and Judean History*, pp. 246-252.

[11] On the vexed question of the "archaeological invisibility" of nomads there has been much recent discussion. For orientation see Finkelstein, *Living on the Fringe: The Archaeology and History of the Negev, Sinai and Neighboring Regions in the Bronze and Middle Ages* (Sheffield: Sheffield Academic Press, 1995), pp. 16-30 and full references there; cf. also R. Cribb, *Nomads in Archaeology* (Cambridge, UK: Cambridge University Press, 1991).

[12] E. Anati, *Har Karkom: The Mountain of God* (New York: Rizzoli Publications, 1986).

[13] E. Oren, "The 'Ways of Horus' in North Sinai," in *Egypt, Israel, Sinai: Archaeological and Historical Relationships in the Biblical Period*, ed. A.F. Rainey (Tel Aviv: Tel Aviv University, 1987), pp. 69-119.

[14] M. Dothan, "The Fortress at Kadesh-Barnea," *Israel Exploration Journal* 15 (1965), pp. 134-151.

[15] R. Cohen, *Kadesh-Barnea: A Fortress from the Time of the Judaean Kingdom* (Jerusalem: Israel Museum, 1983).

[16] L.T. Geraty, "Heshbon: The First Casualty in the Israelite Quest for the Kingdom of God," in *The Quest for the Kingdom of God: Essays in Honor of George E. Mendenhall*, ed. A Green, H.B. Hoffman, and F.A. Spina (Winona Lake, IN: Eisenbrauns, 1983), pp. 239-248.

[17] R. Dornemann, *The Archaeology of Transjordan in the Bronze and Iron Ages* (Milwaukee: Milwaukee Public Museum, 1983), pp. 45, 63; I.A. Sauer, "Transjordan in the Bronze and Iron Ages: A Critique of Glueck's Synthesis," *Bulletin of the American Schools of Oriental Research* 263 (1986), pp. 8-18.

[18] Dornemann, *Archaeology of Transjordan*, p. 34-35.

[19] For the evidence see Sauer, "Critique," pp. 6-14; Dornemann, *Archaeology of Transjordan*, pp. 20-24.

[20] R. Giveon, *Les bédouins Shosou in des documents Égyptiens* (Leiden: Brill, 1971); D.C. Hopkins, "Pastoralists in Late Bronze Age Palestine: Which Way Did They Go?" *Biblical Archaeologist* 56:4 (1993), pp. 200-211.

[21] Dornemann, *Archaeology of Transjordan*, p. 63; Sauer, "Critique," pp. 10, 15, 16; cf. also P. Bienkowski, ed., *Early Edom and Moab: The Beginning of the Iron Age in Southern Jordan* (Sheffield: Sheffield Academic Press, 1992), passim, esp. p. 1-2 and references there.

[22] Dornemann, *Archaeology of Transjordan*, pp. 47, 63; Sauer, "Critique," pp. 14-15.

[23] R.G. Boling, *The Early Biblical Community in Transjordan* (Sheffield: Almond Press, 1988), is an anachronism, a curious throwback to the now defunct school of "biblical archaeology," whose amateurism, bias, and distorted use of archaeological data has discredited it, even in most biblical circles. For a far superior treatment of Transjordan in the Late Bronze/Iron I transition, see Bienkowski, *Edom and Moab*.

[24] See references in n. 21, above.

[25] Elsewhere I have refuted the "secular Fundamentalism" of Zertal; see Zertal, "Israel Enters Canaan—Following the Pottery Trail," *Biblical Archaeology Review* 17:5 (1991), pp. 28-49, 75. See Dever, "Cultural Continuity, Ethnicity in the Archaeological Community, and the Question of Israelite Origins," *Eretz-Israel* 24 (1993), pp. 22*-33*.

[26] See n. 25, above, and n. 38, below.

[27] For recent critiques of Albright, see several articles in *Biblical Archaeologist* 56:1 (1993), including my "What Remains of the House That Albright Built?" pp. 25-36.

[28] Y. Yadin, "The Transition from a Semi-Nomadic to a Sedentary Society in the Twelfth Century B.C.E.," in *Symposia Celebrating the Seventy-fifth Anniversary of the American Schools of Oriental Research*, ed. F.M. Cross (Cambridge, MA: American Schools of Oriental Research, 1979), pp. 57-70; cf. Y. Aharoni, "New Aspects of the Israelite Occupation in the North," in *Near Eastern Archaeology in the Twentieth Century*, ed. J.A. Sanders (Garden City, NY: Doubleday, 1970), pp. 254-265.

[29] See references in n. 3, above.

[30] Finkelstein, *Israelite Settlement*.

[31] See Yadin, "Transition"; renewed excavations at Hazor under the direction of A. Ben-Tor have brought to light much more evidence of a 13th-century B.C.E. destruction, but its date remains unclear and may be considerably earlier than Yadin's date of c. 1225 B.C.E. (i.e., Israelite).

[32] A. Biran, *Biblical Dan* (Jerusalem: Israel Exploration Society, 1994), pp. 125, 126.

[33] L. Toombs, "Shechem: Problems of the Early Israelite Era," in Cross, *Symposia*, pp. 63-83.

[34] On the rise of the Israelite state, with full references to the literature, see my "Archaeology and the 'Age of Solomon': A Case-study in Archaeology and Historiography," in *The Age of Solomon: Scholarship at the Turn of the Millennium*, ed. L.T. Handy (Leiden: Brill, forthcoming).

[35] Finkelstein, *Israelite Settlement*; Zertal, "Israel Enters Canaan."

[36] D.L. Esse, "The Collared Rim Jar at Megiddo: Ceramic Distribution and Ethnicity," *Journal of Near Eastern Studies* 51:2 (1992), pp. 81-103.

[37] L.E. Stager, "The Archaeology of the Family in Ancient Israel," *Bulletin of the American Schools of Oriental Research* 260 (1985), pp. 1-35.

[38] The question of "ethnicity in the archaeological record" is hotly debated today. Cf. Dever, "Cultural Continuity"; and Finkelstein and Na'aman, *From Nomadism to Monarchy*, pp. 164-171. See also Finkelstein, "Pots and Peoples Revisited: Ethnic Boundaries in the Iron Age," in *The Archaeology of Israel: Constructing the Past/Interpreting the Present*, ed. D. Small and N.A. Silberman (Sheffield: Sheffield Academic Press, 1997); and cf. my forth-coming reply, "Israelite Origins and the 'Nomadic Ideal': Can Archaeology Separate Fact from Fiction?"

[39] A full-scale examination of the Late Bronze-Iron I transition in the eastern Mediterranean—long a desideratum—has now appeared in W.A. Ward and M.S. Joukowsky, eds., *The Twelfth Century B.C.: From Beyond the Danube to the Tigris* (Dubuque, IA: Kendall/Hunt Publishing, 1992); cf. my chapter in the same volume, "The Late Bronze-Early Iron I Horizon in Syria-Palestine: Egyptians, Canaanites, 'Sea Peoples,' and 'Proto-Israelites,'" pp. 99-110.

[40] For orientation on the "New Literary Criticism," see the essays in J.C. Exum and D.J.A. Clines, eds., *The New Literary Criticism and the Hebrew Bible* (Sheffield: JSOT Press, 1993). Asking only *how* the texts "signify," however, seems to beg the question of historicity.

[41] Cf. R. Polzin, *Moses and the Deuteronomist: A Literary Study of the Deuteronomic History* (New York: Seabury Press, 1980); Gottwald, *The Hebrew Bible: A Socio-Literary Introduction* (Philadelphia: Fortress Press, 1985).

[42] Gottwald, *Hebrew Bible*, p. 258.

[43] B. Halpern, "The Exodus from Egypt: Myth or Reality?" in *The Rise of Ancient Israel*, ed. Shanks (Washington, DC: Biblical Archaeology Society, 1992), pp. 86-113.

[44] Cf. Redford, in Rainey, *Egypt, Israel, Sinai*, pp. 41-56; cf. also Redford, in this volume.

5

EXODUS AND ARCHAEOLOGICAL REALITY

James Weinstein

T he cynic might claim that nothing new has been learned about the departure of the Children of Israel from Egypt since the last redaction of the Old Testament. While many people might consider such a statement an unduly harsh assessment of the situation, the archaeological record has revealed little to dispute its validity. Today, after more than a century of archaeological research in Egypt and Palestine, nothing has been found that can be directly linked to either the biblical account of the sojourn in Egypt or a large-scale migration by the Children of Israel out of that country.

The opposite situation is of course true in regard to the Israelite settlement. Since the late 1960s, surveys and excavations in Israel, Jordan, and the West Bank—especially in the central highlands—have shed considerable light on the development of early Israelite settlements in the 12th and 11th centuries B.C.[1] This research has forced an abandonment of the conquest and peasant revolt models for the early history of the Israelites in Canaan (at least for the late 13th and 12th centuries B.C.) and has demonstrated the importance of environmental, ecological, and socioeconomic data for analyzing early Israelite society.

These investigations have also provided an interesting piece of information for Egyptologists and others concerned with the possible historicity of the Exodus. The material culture of the early Iron Age settlements in the central highlands and closely adjoining areas (the regions where early Israelite society appears to have developed most intensely) reveals few signs of contact with Egypt—certainly nothing that would lead one to suppose that the inhabitants of these places had any Egyptian heritage. Egyptian artifacts are conspicuous by their rarity or absence at these sites, and at those places where they have been found they are limited to a few small objects (mostly scarabs and other small items) that could have been acquired almost anywhere and by almost any means.[2]

Among the Egyptian finds in this category are two design scarabs,[3] possibly from the lower of two strata associated with an early Iron Age structure found on Mt. Ebal, a few kilometers north of ancient Shechem.[4] The base of one scarab displays a complex design dominated by a rosette pattern. Brandl cites several parallels for this design; all but one are from contexts contemporary with the XIXth Dynasty, the period he favors for the date of the scarab.[5] Brandl mentions a single excavated parallel for the design on the second scarab, which shows a squatting archer facing a cartouche containing the prenomen of Thutmose III.[6] The parallel appears on a seal from Tomb 935 at Tell el-Farʿah (S.), a tomb that also contained several seals inscribed with the name of Ramesses II. Whether the date of manufacture of the two Mt. Ebal scarabs is contemporary with that site or somewhat earlier is uncertain. Zertal and Brandl employ the scarabs to date the founding of this site to the second half of the 13th century B.C., a conclusion followed by Finkelstein.[7] Parallels for the ceramic corpus of Stratum II belong in the 12th century B.C., however, and the attribution of the two scarabs to Stratum II seems less than a certainty;[8] hence, there is little reason to favor the late-13th-century B.C. date over the early 12th century B.C. for the beginning of the Mt. Ebal site. Precise dating of the Mt. Ebal building on the basis of the two design scarabs is not feasible.

Another scarab from a settlement attributed to the early Israelites is a single design scarab from Stratum II at ʿIzbet Sartah, located on the western edge of the Shephelah. Giveon's publication of this object notes a parallel for the seated lion dominating the base of the scarab on a seal from Tomb 934 at Tell el-Farʿah (S.),[9] which also contained materials of the XIXth and early XXth Dynasties (down to the reign of Ramesses IV).[10] Since the excavator's date for Stratum II at ʿIzbet Sartah is the late 11th century B.C. (a date also favored by Dever),[11] the scarab has no value for dating the beginning of the settlement period.

Another item perhaps reflecting an Egyptian connection is a scarab impression on the handle of a collar-rim jar from Stratum V (late 12th-early 11th century B.C.) at Shiloh.[12] The partially preserved design on the impression shows a walking lion, a simple motif with a long history in Egypt and the Levant during the second and first millennia B.C.

The paucity and cultural insignificance of the Egyptian and Egyptianizing finds from early Iron Age sites linked to the Israelites is notable. A recent article by Menakhem Shuval[13] on early Iron Age stamp seals (including scarabs, plaques, bullae, conoids, seal impressions, etc.) reinforces the evidence obtained from the other archaeological sources. Shuval discerns three regionally distinct groups of seals. The first group is from sites in the Jezreel Valley and northward and displays connections with Syria and other northern regions. The second group is from sites in the south and on the coastal plain and shows many connections with Egypt. The third group is from highland sites; the sphragistic developments in this region are largely indigenous to the area but also show some connections to sites to the east (e.g., Sahab in Jordan) and to the north. There is little evidence of Egyptian influence in the seals from the highlands. The seal data certainly support the view that the inhabitants of the hill country sites lacked a Nilotic background and that their culture developed quite independently of that of Egypt.

Some might assert that the sparsity of evidence for Egyptian contacts with early Iron Age sites associated with the Israelites supports the Bible's silence on Egypt during the "Conquest period" and thus is negative evidence for the historicity of the Exodus narrative. In the early 12th century B.C., however, Israelite settlements were not widespread outside the central hill country and the Galilee, and they were few in number in the south (where they appear to concentrate in the Beersheba Valley). That would argue for a hill country or even eastern background for the Israelites, not southern Canaan and, ultimately, Egypt.

One possibly early attestation of Israelites in the Beersheba Valley is at Tel Masos. There, Egyptian influence has been identified in Stratum II in architectural elements such as the tripartite layout of House 480, which is reminiscent of houses at Amarna and House 1500 at Beth Shan (House 480 was initially constructed at the time of the previous level, Stratum IIIA),[14] and in a bit of Egyptian pottery, specifically, two Ramesside "flower pots."[15] A scarab whose design displays a pair of quadrupeds was also found in Stratum II.[16]

Giveon has interpreted a scarab found on the surface of the site[17] as displaying part of the prenomen of Sety II, though Brandl[18] has suggested that the name may be that of Ramesses X of the late XXth Dynasty. The lack of a stratified context for the scarab makes it impossible to determine when the object may have reached the site. Moreover, there is no inherent reason why the signs on the base must be read as part of a royal name. The scarab contains only two hieroglyphic signs, $ḥpr$ and r^c. Efforts to read the inscription on this object as part of the prenomen of Sety II ($wsr-ḥpr(w)-r^c$) or Ramesses X ($ḥpr-m3^ct-r^c$), rather than as an epithet, are not convincing. The occurrence of two signs on a scarab that contains a representation of a king smiting his enemy does not necessarily indicate the presence of a royal name. That certainly is the case with scarabs of this type which have two signs that do not form part of any known royal name[19] and is probably also the situation with many other scarabs of this genre. In my opinion, the chronological and historical significance of the Tel Masos scarab has been overblown. In general, we should refrain from identifying such scarabs as royal-name items unless they contain the full complement of hieroglyphic signs or have some typological feature that is distinctive of the scarabs naming a particular pharaoh.

Some doubt attaches to the identification of Tel Masos as an Israelite site.[20] If it is Israelite (which most scholars agree it is), it is unlike contemporary Israelite settlements further north in several respects, one of which is the occurrence of the Egyptian architectural features. Lest one think that the presence of some Egyptian architectural influence, two pots, and two scarabs supports the notion of an Egyptian origin for the settlers at Tel Masos, however, it must be emphasized that many sites in southern Palestine in the late second millennium B.C. reveal Egyptian elements, a legacy of the substantial Egyptian military and administrative presence in the region during the 13th and first half of the 12th centuries B.C. Moreover, since no Egyptian artifacts are stratigraphically linked to the initial phase of occupation at the site (Stratum IIIB), one should not relate the earliest occupants of Tel Masos to Egypt.

During the Ramesside period, Egyptian military and administrative activity in Canaan centered on the coastal plain, the western half of the northern Negev, the Jezreel and Huleh valleys, and perhaps also on parts of the Jordan Valley. Early Israelite settlements, however, were concentrated in regions with which the Egyptians had only limited political or military interest. It is not surprising, therefore, that Egyptian artifacts and cultural influence are common at lowland Canaanite sites such as Megiddo, Gezer, and Beth Shan as well as at Philistine sites such as Ashkelon, Tel Miqne, and Tell Qasile. The distribution of material culture finds indicates that Egypt's principal interests in the 12th and 11th centuries were with the Philistines, other Sea Peoples, and lowland Canaanites rather than with the Israelites. Interactions between the Egyptians and the early Israelites appear to have been very limited.

Such an observation may find further support in the evidence provided by the Karnak reliefs, which Frank Yurco, Donald Redford, and Anson Rainey have discussed in considerable detail.[21] Their debate over the significance of these scenes—whether they reflect a military encounter between the Egyptians and "Israelites" in a hilly region in the reign of Merenptah or that of Ramesses II, and whether the Israelites the Egyptian forces clashed with were Shasu or Canaanites—is interesting from the perspective of identifying the occupants of the early Israelite settlements and the historicity of Merenptah's "Israel" Stela, but it is not relevant to the question of an exodus from Egypt. The Karnak reliefs and the Merenptah Stela may point toward the time and general location of an Egyptian military encounter with early Israelites, but they say nothing about a possible Egyptian origin for these people.[22] Moreover, the inhabitants of the earliest Israelite settlements in the highlands were relatively few in number (based on surveys and excavated late-13th- to early-12th-century B.C. sites), and they appear to have been an insignificant lot militarily, compared to their urbanized Canaanite and Philistine contemporaries; hence, one cannot be certain that they are the same people as those named in the Merenptah Stela. It is quite possible that the Israelites in the Karnak reliefs (assuming the scene does represent these people) and the Merenptah Stela were nonurbanized Canaanites or Shasu[23] from the low, rolling hills of the Shephelah or the Galilee rather than the occupants of the small highland settlements.

In summary, the meager Egyptian finds at early Israelite sites as well as the Karnak reliefs and the Merenptah Stela provide no data that would bolster the historical validity of the biblical account of an exodus from Egypt. They certainly do not support the notion of a 13th- or early-12th-century B.C. Israelite "conquest" of Canaan, nor the claim that the people "Israel" named in Merenptah's Stela was a "geographically extensive tribal coalition by the late thirteenth century B.C."[24]

The reactions of some religious conservatives to the recent archaeological discoveries have not been unexpected. A few simply ignore the archaeological data and continue the hunt for ever more signs of Semitic peoples in Egypt during the New Kingdom. Such an approach, however, can never demonstrate the historicity of the Exodus. One cannot use the discovery of a new literary parallel between the Old Testament and an Egyptian text, or yet another "scientific" or "natural" explanation for one of the biblical plagues or the "Miracle of the Sea," or the identification of more Semitic names and Levantine material culture items in XVIIIth and XIXth Dynasty Egyptian contexts, to postulate an exodus. Nor does it really matter whether the Egyptian place names in the biblical account are truly Ramesside in origin or, as Redford has posited, more appropriate to the Saite and Persian periods.[25] And it makes little difference how many Asiatic prisoners Sety I, Ramesses II, or even Ramesses III brought back from Canaan compared to their predecessors.[26] The only question that *really* matters is whether any (nonbiblical) textual or archaeological materials indicate a major outflow of Asiatics from Egypt to Canaan at any point in the XIXth or even early XXth Dynasty. And so far the answer to that question is no.

The effort by some scholars to transfer the date of the Exodus from the 13th century B.C. back to the late 15th century B.C. is even more insupportable on archaeological grounds. This earlier date maintains a biblical linkage to the Exodus by relating the alleged event to the reference in 1 Kings 6 to the Exodus having taken place 480 years prior to the start of construction of the Solomonic Temple in Jerusalem. Recent champions of this theory include John Bimson and Bryant Wood. Bimson's efforts[27] to date the destructions of Middle Bronze Age towns to the late 15th century B.C. are flawed by a host of Egyptological, stratigraphic, and chronological problems, and to date, no Syro-Palestinian archaeologists or Egyptologists have accepted his chronological and historical analysis of the data. As for Wood, his argument is based on a redating of the destruction at Jericho from the 16th century B.C. to the end of the 15th century B.C. and suffers from a number of serious deficiencies in the interpretation of the archaeological and radiocarbon evidence.[28]

One explanation offered by historians and archaeologists for the biblical Exodus is an Israelite folk memory of the Hyksos expulsion from the eastern delta in the third quarter of the 16th century B.C.[29] This "Hyksos interpretation" has several advantages over other explanations. It has a large, mostly Semitic group departing Egypt from the right area (the eastern delta), according to the biblical report, and it places the Exodus in the same century as the destruction and abandonment of numerous Canaanite towns if one wants to relate at least some of the devastation to the fleeing Hyksos/Hebrews.[30] And if one wishes to believe the account preserved in Josephus, the Hyksos went up into Judea, founding a city they called Jerusalem, thus placing them in the same approximate area as many of the early, though considerably post-Hyksos period, Israelite settlements.

Yet it needs to be recognized that Manfred Bietak's excavations at Tell el-Dabʿa (ancient Avaris) cause more than a bit of difficulty for the notion of a large-scale migration from Egypt by Asiatics in the 16th century B.C. True, much of Tell el-Dabʿa was abandoned at the beginning of the XVIIIth Dynasty, after its capture by Ahmose.[31] The question is, Where did the majority of the inhabitants of this large urban center go? If they remained in Egypt, it would be difficult to trace them in the archaeological record because by the end of the Second Intermediate Period their culture was highly Egyptianized—in many respects almost indistinguishable from that of their Egyptian contemporaries. If they migrated back to Canaan in large numbers, it might be possible to detect the intrusion of this Egyptianized population in the indigenous late MB IIC-early LB I Canaanite cultural matrix.

As it turns out, one looks in vain for a substantial influx of Egyptian material culture features into late-16th-century B.C. Palestine. In fact, just the opposite situation seems to be true in most areas of the country. The southern Levant at the beginning of the Late Bronze Age remained heavily Canaanite in character, with a decline, not an increase, in the number of Egyptian imports from the previous MB IIC period. Analysis of the pottery, scarabs, and beads reveals a continuation of Middle Bronze Age features, with little indication of a major infusion of Nilotic elements.[32] Tell el-ʿAjjul reveals considerable Egyptian influence in this period, but it stands out as an exception to the general phenomenon of limited material contacts between Egypt and Palestine during the late 16th century B.C. Certainly, the richness of Tell el-ʿAjjul at this time would be quite understandable if it was the site of Hyksos Sharuhen—though even at Tell el-ʿAjjul the town suffered a substantial population decline in the LB I period following a massive destruction.[33] In summary, there is no evidence for the influx of a large population from Egypt into Canaan at the transition from the Middle Bronze Age to the Late Bronze Age.

The counterargument to this position—that archaeologists simply have not discovered the sites at which the Egyptian materials might be found—is weak. Surveys have been conducted along the principal route across the northern Sinai as well as in the northern Negev and the southern Shephelah, and excavations have been undertaken at a number of these sites. Oren found that the principal periods of activity across the northern Sinai during the second millennium B.C. were in the XVIIIth Dynasty and then again in Ramesside times.[34] A small number of sites of Middle Kingdom date were also detected, but there was no sign of activity during the Second Intermediate Period. In the northern Sinai, as in Palestine, there is no indication of a large increase in Egyptian material culture finds or influence datable to the 16th century B.C. As for the increase in Egyptian activity in the 13th and 12th centuries B.C., that relates to the well-documented XIXth and early XXth Dynasty Egyptian military and administrative presence in the region.

The archaeological materials in the northern and western Negev, while less well known, also fail to indicate a movement of large numbers of new residents into this area in the 16th century B.C. In fact, destructions, abandonments, and/or considerable declines in population characterize the Middle Bronze Age-Late Bronze Age transition at such sites as Tell Abu Hureira, Tell el-Far'ah (S.), and as noted above, Tell el-'Ajjul.[35] As for Tell esh-Shari'a, a late MB IIC-early LB I occupation appears at that site in Stratum XII, apparently without any destruction or abandonment.[36] It is not possible to say from the minimal evidence published so far, however, whether that occupation predates or postdates the beginning of the XVIIIth Dynasty.

These data raise the question of whether the bulk of the Egyptianized Asiatic population of Avaris ever left Egypt or simply abandoned Tell el-Dab'a and other Hyksos sites and moved elsewhere in the delta and farther south. Textual and archaeological evidence on this matter is lacking. In the absence of an adequate number of surveys and excavations covering a wide area of the delta, one can say little about the ultimate destination of the Asiatic residents of the eastern delta. Perhaps the last of the Hyksos rulers, Khamudy, moved with members of his court from Avaris back to southern Canaan. Many other Asiatics probably remained in Egypt, however, gradually blending into the native Egyptian population.

Perhaps an alternative explanation for the biblical narrative is to be found in the abandonment of the Asiatic occupations at eastern delta sites such as Tell el-Maskhuta and possibly Tell el-Yahudiya. Those occupations, which seem to have been less Egyptianized than urban Avaris, saw a decline or abandonment about 1600 B.C. or shortly thereafter, at a period roughly contemporary with Jericho tomb groups IV and V.[37] Perhaps the inhabitants of some of these sites moved inside the walls of fortified towns such as Avaris, which saw a consolidation of population in the late Second Intermediate Period.[38] Other pastoralists and agriculturalists, however, may have wandered back to Palestine, to merge with similar groups living on the fringes of urban Canaan.

In recent years there has been a general reassessment of the situation in 16th-century B.C. Palestine, with a number of archaeologists and historians arguing against Egyptian involvement in the many destructions and abandonments (other than at a few towns near the southern coast, perhaps). Some of these scholars propose environmental or ecological causes for supposed political, economic, or population distortions that resulted in civil unrest among the local population and, ultimately, military conflict and the collapse of the Middle Bronze Age towns.[39] As yet, however, there is little evidence for any environmental crisis in Palestine at the end of the Middle Bronze Age.[40] Another view, to attribute the destructions and abandonments to a Hurrian or Mitannian movement from Syria, seems highly unlikely for southernmost Palestine, the area of greatest devastation and abandonment, as there is no archaeological or textual evidence for Hurrians in this region during the 16th century B.C.[41] Yet another theory involves the possibility of a combination of interurban warfare and Asiatics migrating back to Palestine from Egypt.[42] But there is no evidence in the archaeological record for either a large-scale Asiatic migration back to Palestine or the participation of those Asiatics in the urban disaster that hit Palestine in the 16th century B.C.

CONCLUSIONS

There is no archaeological evidence for an exodus such as is described in the Bible in any period within the second millennium B.C. Perhaps there was a migration of Semites out of Egypt in the late 13th or early 12th century B.C., but if such an event did take place, the number of people involved was so small that no trace is likely to be

identified in the archaeological record. Indeed, Israel Finkelstein's estimates that the *total* Israelite population west of the Jordan River in the
mid to late 12th century B.C. may have been as little as about 21,000—and
only slightly more than about 40,000 (or, at most, 55,000) at the end of the
11th or early 10th century B.C.[43]—would, if even remotely correct, allow
for the migration of perhaps several hundred Asiatics at most. If there
was an historical exodus, it probably consisted of a small number of
Semites migrating out of Egypt in the late 13th or early 12th century B.C.,
ultimately settling in southwestern Canaan, where their Egyptian heritage would allow them to melt into the local populace without leaving
anything to permit us to identify them as a distinctive group. But even if
such an event did take place, the impact of these immigrants on the material culture of the Israelite settlements in the hill country in the 12th and
11th centuries B.C. would have been minimal. Were it not for the Bible,
anyone looking at the Palestinian archaeological data today would con-
clude that whatever the origin of the Israelites, it was not Egypt.

One can choose to believe or disbelieve the Old Testament report of
an exodus on a variety of religious and/or secular grounds. The account
of a mass migration out of Egypt by the Children of Israel was of
immense importance to the ancient Israelites, and it continues to exert
great fascination for students and scholars of the Old Testament as well
as the lay public. All the same, unless new and better evidence for this
"event" is forthcoming, the Exodus story cannot be considered a topic
for productive archaeological research.

ENDNOTES

[1] This paper follows Finkelstein's identification of the Iron Age settlements in the southern
and central hill country of Palestine as Israelite; see I. Finkelstein, *The Archaeology of the
Israelite Settlement* (Jerusalem: Israel Exploration Society, 1988), pp. 27-33. Likewise, the
designation of ʿIzbet Sartah as an Israelite site follows Finkelstein. It is recognized, however, that such identifications are based mostly on later biblical traditions regarding the

location of early Israelite settlements, rather than on any specific archaeological data, as pointed out so well by Herzog in his discussion of the early Iron Age settlements in the Beersheba Valley; see Z. Herzog, "The Beer-Sheba Valley: From Nomadism to Monarchy," in *From Nomadism to Monarchy: Archaeological and Historical Aspects of Early Israel*, ed. Finkelstein and N. Na'aman (Jerusalem: Israel Exploration Society, 1994).

[2] A very early date for the Exodus, in the late 3d millennium B.C., has been proposed by Anati ("Has Mt. Sinai Been Found?" *Biblical Archaeology Review* 11:4 [1985], pp. 42-57, and *The Mountain of God* [New York: Rizzoli, 1986]). Reconciliation of this date with the archaeological and textual data from Egypt, or with the evidence of the early Israelite settlements in Palestine, is impossible; cf. W.H. Stiebing, Jr., "Should the Exodus and the Israelite Settlement Be Redated?" *Biblical Archaeology Review* 11:4 (1985), pp. 58-69.

[3] B. Brandl, "Two Scarabs and a Trapezoidal Seal from Mount Ebal," *Tel Aviv* 13-14 (1986-1987), pp. 166-172.

[4] See A. Zertal, "Has Joshua's Altar Been Found on Mt. Ebal?" *Biblical Archaeology Review* 11:1 (1985), p. 42, "How Can Kempinski Be So Wrong?" *Biblical Archaeology Review* 12:1 (1986), pp. 52, 53, and "'To the Land of the Perizzites and the Giants': On the Israelite Settlement in the Hill Country of Manasseh," in Finkelstein and Na'aman, *From Nomadism to Monarchy*, pp. 61-66. For doubts as to whether this site should be considered Israelite, see M.D. Coogan, "Of Cults and Cultures: Reflections on the Interpretation of Archaeological Evidence," *Palestine Exploration Quarterly* 119 (1987), pp. 1-8.

[5] O. Keel ("Früheisenzeitliche Glyptik in Palästina/Israel," in O. Keel, M. Shuval, and C. Uehlinger, *Studien zu den Stempelsiegeln aus Palästina/Israel*, vol. 3, Orbis Biblicus et Orientalis 100 [Freiburg/Göttingen: Universitätsverlag/Vandenhoeck & Ruprecht, 1990], pp. 351-353) allows for a somewhat later dating of the item.

[6] Keel ("Früheisenzeitliche Glyptik," p. 351) reads the prenomen as a cryptographic writing of the name of the god Amun.

[7] Finkelstein, *Israelite Settlement*, p. 321.

[8] See, e.g., Finkelstein, *Israelite Settlement*, pp. 85, 321; cf. Zertal, "An Early Iron Age Cultic Site on Mount Ebal: Excavation Seasons 1982-1987," *Tel Aviv* 13-14 (1986-1987), pp. 115-118.

[9] R. Giveon, "An Egyptian Scarab of the 20th Dynasty," in Finkelstein, *'Izbet Ṣarṭah: An Early Iron Age Site near Rosh Ha'ayin, Israel*, British Archaeological Reports, International Series 299 (1986), pp. 104-105.

[10] E. Macdonald, J.L. Starkey, and L. Harding, *Beth-Pelet II*, British School of Archaeology in Egypt and Egyptian Research Account 52 (London: British School of Archaeology in Egypt/Bernard Quaritch, 1932), pl. 52:129. Keel's efforts ("Früheisenzeitliche Glyptik," pp. 348-350) to obtain a cryptographic writing of the name Amun from the three signs on this seal are not convincing.

[11] W.G. Dever, "Archaeological Data on the Israelite Settlement: A Review of Two Recent Works," *Bulletin of the American Schools of Oriental Research* 284 (1991), p. 78.

[12] S. Bunimovitz, in Finkelstein, Bunimovitz, and Z. Lederman, *Shiloh: The Archaeology of a Biblical Site*, Monograph Series of the Institute of Archaeology, Tel Aviv University 10 (Tel Aviv: Institute of Archaeology, Tel Aviv University, 1993), pp. 215-216, fig. 8:14.

[13] Shuval, "A Catalogue of Early Iron Stamp Seals from Israel," in Keel, Shuval, and Uehlinger, *Stempelsiegeln*.

[14] V. Fritz and A. Kempinski, *Ergebnisse der Ausgrabungen auf der Ḥirbet el-Mšāš (Tēl Māśōś)*,

1972-1975, 3 vols. (Wiesbaden: Harrassowitz, 1983), pp. 61-67; E.D. Oren, "'Governors' Residencies' in Canaan under the New Kingdom: A Case Study of Egyptian Administration," *Journal of the Society for the Study of Egyptian Antiquities* 14 (1984), pp. 48-49; Herzog, "Beer-Sheba Valley," pp. 128-129.

[15] Fritz and Kempinski, *Ḥirbet el-Mšāš*, pp. 21, 78, pls. 134:4, 151:7.

[16] Fritz and Kempinski, *Ḥirbet el-Mšāš*, pp. 105-106, pls. 107:2, 170:3.

[17] Giveon, "A Monogram Scarab from Tel Masos," *Tel Aviv* 1 (1974), pp. 75-76; Fritz and Kempinski, *Ḥirbet el-Mšāš*, pp. 102-105, pls. 107C, 170:2; back and profile shown in Keel, "Früheisenzeitliche Glyptik," fig. 17.

[18] Brandl, "The Tel Masos Scarab: A Suggestion for a New Method for the Interpretation of Royal Scarabs," *Scripta Hierosolymitana* 28 (1982), pp. 371-405.

[19] See, e.g., the *wsr* and *nfr* signs on the smiting pharaoh scarab from Langada, Cos, in L. Morricone, "Eleona e Langada: Sepolcreti della tarda Età del Bronzo a Coo," *Annuario della Scuola Archeologica di Atene e delle Missioni Italiane in Oriente* 43-44, n.s. 27-28 (1965-1966), fig. 244. Note also the *r ʿ* and *t3wy* signs in front of the smiting pharaoh on a scarab that has two additional signs behind the king, in E. Hornung and E. Staehelin, eds., *Skarabäen und andere Siegelamulette aus Basler Sammlungen*, Ägyptische Denkmäler in der Schweiz 1 (Mainz: Philipp von Zabern, 1976), no. 309, cf. no. 308.

[20] For recent discussions see Finkelstein, *Israelite Settlement*, pp. 45-46; Dever, "Archaeology and Israelite Origins: Review Article," *Bulletin of the American Schools of Oriental Research* 279 (1990), pp. 94-95, and "Archaeological Data," p. 87; Herzog, "Beer-Sheba Valley," pp. 146-148.

[21] F. Yurco, "Merenptah's Canaanite Campaign," *Journal of the American Research Center in Egypt* 23 (1986), pp. 189-215, "3,200-Year-Old Picture of Israelites Found in Egypt," *Biblical Archaeology Review* 16:5 (1990), pp. 20-38, and "Yurco's Response," *Biblical Archaeology Review* 17:6 (1991), p. 61; D.B. Redford, "The Ashkelon Relief at Karnak and the Israel Stela," *Israel Exploration Journal* 36 (1986), pp. 188-200; A.F. Rainey, "Rainey's Challenge," *Biblical Archaeology Review* 17:6 (1991), pp. 56-60, 93.

[22] Recent efforts by G. Rendsburg ("The Date of the Exodus and the Conquest/Settlement: The Case for the 1100s," *Vetus Testamentum* 42 [1992], pp. 510-527) to lower the date of the Exodus to the 12th century B.C. and to identify the Israelites in the Merenptah Stela as slaves still living in Egypt are unpersuasive. Rendsburg's "positive approach to the biblical account of an Exodus" (p. 512) pushes that "event" down into the 12th century in order to reconcile the biblical account with the destructions and occupations at certain Palestinian sites in that later period. That, in turn, causes him to identify the pharaoh of the Exodus as Ramesses III. Flaws in Rendsburg's theory include the lack of any indication in the Merenptah Stela that the people named "Israel" in that text were in Egypt, the impossibility of reconciling those destructions that took place in the 13th century with a migration that supposedly did not occur until the 12th century, and the absence of any indication of an Egyptian background for the inhabitants of the early Israelite settlements.

[23] It is not clear why the Israelites of the Old Testament must have arisen out of only one Late Bronze Age ethnic group. There is enough diversity among the remains associated with early Israelite settlements in Palestine to suggest that these people, though perhaps linked by certain shared religious beliefs, emanated from more than one Late Bronze Age population.

[24] J. Bimson, "Merenptah's Israel and Recent Theories of Israelite Origins," *Journal for the Study of the Old Testament* 49 (1991), pp. 3-29.

[25] Redford, "An Egyptological Perspective on the Exodus Narrative," in *Egypt, Israel, Sinai:*

Archaeological and Historical Relationships in the Biblical Period, ed. Rainey (Tel Aviv: Tel Aviv University, 1987), pp. 137-161, and Egypt, Canaan, and Israel in Ancient Times (Princeton: Princeton University Press, 1992), pp. 409-410. For a harsh response to Redford's position, see K.A. Kitchen, review of Egypt, Israel, Sinai, by Rainey, in Journal of Egyptian Archaeology 77 (1991), pp. 205-206; see also M. Bietak, "Comments on the 'Exodus,'" in Rainey, Egypt, Israel, Sinai, pp. 163-171.

26 Bietak ("An Iron Age Four-Room House in Ramesside Egypt," Eretz-Israel 23 [1992], pp. 10*-12*) has pointed out that a late Ramesside period house excavated years ago in western Thebes shows some architectural similarities to the typical Iron Age I four-room house. This structure may (or may not) provide additional evidence for the presence of Asiatics in Egypt during the late 12th or early 11th century B.C., but it has no obvious relevance to an exodus.

27 Bimson, Redating the Exodus and Conquest, 2d ed. (Sheffield: Almond Press, 1981).

28 B. Wood, "Did the Israelites Conquer Jericho? A New Look at the Archaeological Evidence," Biblical Archaeology Review 16:2 (1990), pp. 44-58; and "Dating Jericho's Destruction: Bienkowski is Wrong on All Counts," Biblical Archaeology Review 16:5 (1990), pp. 45-49, 68.

The alleged evidence for the redating that Wood relies on includes the pottery associated with the "Middle Bronze Age" destruction debris, a single radiocarbon date (BM-1790) from the destruction, and the presence of a cartouche plaque of Tuthmosis III and a scarab of Hatshepsut in Tomb 5 of Garstang's earlier excavations at the site (J. Garstang, "Jericho: City and Necropolis," University of Liverpool, Annals of Archaeology and Anthropology 20 [1933], pl. 26:1-2, 9 = A. Rowe, A Catalogue of Egyptian Scarabs, Scaraboids, Seals and Amulets in the Palestine Archaeological Museum [Cairo: Imprimerie de l'Institut français d'archéologie orientale, 1936], nos. S.21, 472) to make the claim that the tell at Jericho was not destroyed until well into the Late Bronze I period.

An unfortunate flaw in Wood's argument is his use of a radiocarbon assay that the British Museum laboratory (e.g., M.S. Tite et al., "Preliminary statement on an error in British Museum radiocarbon dates (BM-1700 to BM-2315)," Antiquity 61 [1987], p. 168) had already identified as being part of a large series of systematically defective dates. The revised radiocarbon age for this sample (3300 ± 110 B.P.: S.G.E. Bowman, J. Ambers, and M.N. Leese, "Re-Evaluation of British Museum Radiocarbon Dates Issued Between 1980 and 1984," Radiocarbon 32 [1990], p. 74: BM-1790) is 220 years earlier than the one cited in the original excavation report and used by Wood (3080 ± 40 B.P.) and, when calibrated and turned into a calendrical date, is completely consistent with a traditional dating for the Middle Bronze II remains at Jericho. In any event, it is unacceptable to employ a single radiocarbon assay, without even taking into account the date's standard deviation, for the precise dating of an archaeological event.

A second major problem is Wood's failure to understand that the presence of a few royal-name seals in a single tomb is hardly adequate evidence to postulate a significant and continuous occupation on the mound itself in the 15th century B.C. His view ("Jericho's Destruction," p. 49) that the context of the Hatshepsut scarab should be contemporary with that pharaoh's reign because a scarab containing her name would not have been kept as an heirloom is incorrect. There are at least two other scarabs from Palestine that name Hatshepsut; one comes from a 13th-century B.C. level at Beth Shan (Rowe, Catalogue, no. 471, and The Four Canaanite Temples of Beth-Shan, vol. 1, Publications of the Palestine Section of the Museum of the University of Pennsylvania 2 [Philadelphia: University of Pennsylvania Press, 1940], pl. 36:22; Rowe mistakenly dated this level to the reign of Amenophis III). The other Hatshepsut scarab may have been a surface find at Tel Yitzhaqi: Giveon, Scarabs from Recent Excavations in Israel, Orbis Biblicus et Orientalis 83 (Freiburg/Göttingen: Universitätsverlag/Vandenhoeck & Ruprecht, 1988), no. 122.

In any event, the recent publication of a series of high-precision radiocarbon dates of short-lived samples from the MB IIC destruction phase (H.J. Bruins and J. van der Plicht, "The Exodus Enigma," Nature 382 [1996], pp. 213-214) renders the entire argument moot.

These assays consistently and strongly support a 16th-century B.C. date for the end of MB IIC Jericho and cannot be reconciled with a late-15th-century B.C. destruction.

[29] Redford, "Exodus Narrative," pp. 150-151.

[30] J.M. Weinstein, "The Egyptian Empire in Palestine: A Reassessment," *Bulletin of the American Schools of Oriental Research* 241 (1981), pp. 1-28, and "Egypt and the Middle Bronze IIC/Late Bronze IA Transition in Palestine," *Levant* 23 (1991), pp. 105-115; Dever, "'Hyksos,' Egyptian Destructions, and the End of the Palestinian Middle Bronze Age," *Levant* 22 (1990), pp. 75-81.

[31] See Bietak, "Canaan and Egypt During the Middle Bronze Age," *Bulletin of the American Schools of Oriental Research* 281 (1991), p. 47.
It is not yet clear from the preliminary notices (e.g., Bietak, "Minoan Wall-Paintings unearthed at Ancient Avaris," *Egyptian Archaeology: The Bulletin of the Egypt Exploration Society* 2 [1992], pp. 26-28; J. Leclant and G. Clerq, "Fouilles et travaux en Égypte et au Soudan, 1992-1993," *Orientalia* 63 [1994], pp. 361-362) whether the early XVIIIth Dynasty activity at Ezbet Helmi, at the western end of Tell el-Dab'a, represents a continuation of Hyksos-period occupation by Egyptianized Asiatics or the presence of a different population group.

[32] See, e.g., Weinstein, "Transition in Palestine," p. 112 n. 19.

[33] See, e.g, R. Gonen, *Burial Patterns and Cultural Diversity in Late Bronze Age Canaan,* American Schools of Oriental Research Dissertation Series 7 (Winona Lake, IN: Eisenbrauns, 1992), pp. 119-120, table 31.
In my opinion, Tell Abu Hureira is too far inland to be the site of Sharuhen (contra Rainey, "Sharḥân/Sharuhen—The Problem of Identification," *Eretz-Israel* 24 [1993], pp. 178*-87*).

[34] Oren, "Land Bridge Between Asia and Africa: Archaeology of North Sinai up to the Classical Period," in *Sinai,* ed. B. Rothenberg (Washington, D.C.: Binns, 1979), pp. 181-191.

[35] For Tell Abu Hureira, see Oren et al., "Tel Haror—1988," in *Excavations and Surveys in Israel 1989/1990* (Jerusalem: Israel Antiquities Authority, 1991), p. 73; Oren, "Haror, Tel," in *The New Encyclopedia of Archaeological Excavations in the Holy Land,* ed. E. Stern (New York: Simon & Schuster, 1993), vol. 2, p. 582. For Tell el-Far'ah (S.), see Macdonald, Starkey, and Harding, *Beth-Pelet II,* pp. 27-30.

[36] Oren, "Ziklag—A Biblical City on the Edge of the Negev," *Biblical Archaeologist* 45 (1982), pp. 164-165; cf. "Sera', Tel," in Stern, *New Encyclopedia,* vol. 4, p. 1,330.

[37] For Tell el-Yahudiya, see O. Tufnell, "Graves at Tell el-Yehudiyeh: reviewed after a lifetime," in *Archaeology in the Levant: Essays for Kathleen Kenyon,* ed. R. Moorey and P. Parr (Warminster: Aris & Phillips), pp. 81, 87. The date of the abandonment of Tell el-Maskhuta is based on a study of the scarabs from that site; see Weinstein, "Reflections on the Chronology of Tell el-Dab'a," in *Egypt, the Aegean and the Levant: Interconnections in the Second Millennium BC,* ed. W.V. Davies and L. Schofield (London: British Museum, 1995), pp. 87-88.

[38] Bietak, "Canaan and Egypt," pp. 45-46.

[39] For example, Finkelstein, *Israelite Settlement,* pp. 342-343; Bunimovitz, "Socio-Political Transformations in the Central Hill Country in the Late Bronze-Iron I Transition," in Finkelstein and Na'aman, *From Nomadism to Monarchy,* pp. 181-186.

[40] See, e.g., I. Drori and A. Horowitz, "Tel Lachish: Environment and Subsistence during the Middle Bronze, Late Bronze and Iron Ages," *Tel Aviv* 15-16 (1988-1989), pp. 206-211.

[41] Redford, "The Historical Retrospective at the Beginning of Thutmose III's Annals," in *Festschrift Elmar Edel, 12. März 1979*, ed. M. Görg and E. Pusch, Ägypten und Altes Testament 1 (Bamberg, 1979), and *Ancient Times*, pp. 139-140. Na'aman ("The Hurrians and the End of the Middle Bronze Age in Palestine," *Levant* 26 [1994], pp. 175-187) offers a modified version of the Hurrian thesis. He attributes the destructions in northern Palestine to the Hurrians and the destructions in southern Palestine to the Egyptians, while leaving interior Palestine outside the area of foreign conquest. The principal problem with this interpretation, as I see it, is the chronological gap in evidence for the Hurrians anywhere in Palestine during the 16th century B.C.

[42] P. Bienkowski, *Jericho in the Late Bronze Age* (Warminster: Aris & Phillips, 1986), p. 28.

[43] Finkelstein, *Israelite Settlement*, pp. 332-334. M. Broshi and Finkelstein ("The Population of Palestine in Iron Age II," in *Bulletin of the American Schools of Oriental Research* 287 [1992], p. 55) give a figure of about 65,000 for c. 1000 B.C.

6

SUMMARY AND CONCLUSIONS

William A. Ward

These presentations have focused on the two major components of the biblical Exodus narrative, the Exodus itself and the subsequent conquest of Canaan. Despite the suggestive title of this conference, there is no Egyptian evidence that offers direct testimony to the Exodus as described in the Old Testament. There are hints here and there to indicate that something like an exodus could have happened, though on a vastly smaller scale, but there is not a word in a text or an archaeological artifact that lends credence to the biblical narrative as it now stands. Egypt remains silent, as it always has. From the Egyptian viewpoint, the Old Testament narrative records a series of earthshaking episodes that never happened.

With regard to the Conquest narrative, there has been a major shift away from the traditional view to an alternative founded in measurable, tangible proof. Archaeological and linguistic studies have combined to offer an attractive, though far less heroic, picture of the early Israelites of the Conquest period and have placed them, really for the first time, within a known context and with a recognizable identity. The linguistic evidence was detailed 20 years ago by University of Michigan professor George Mendenhall, though his argument was received with some skepticism at the time. Since then, archaeological discoveries have more than validated the results of linguistic study. This new material has been neatly summed up by Neil Silberman in a recent article entitled "Who Were the Israelites?" published in the journal *Archaeology* (March/April 1992). He states (p. 22):

> A new generation of archaeologists working in Israel has come to challenge the scriptural account in a manner that might seem heretical to some. Their survey, excavation, and analysis of finds from hundreds of Early Iron Age settlements in the rugged hill country of the West Bank and Galilee have led them to conclude that the ancient Israelite confederacy did not arise in a divinely directed military conquest from the desert but through a remarkable socio-economic change in the lives of a few thousand herders, farmers, and villagers in Canaan itself.

While Silberman is here speaking of an alternative to Joshua's conquest, that narrative cannot be separated from the story of the Exodus. As has been stated forcefully here today, if there was no conquest, there is no need for the Exodus.

It is useful to look briefly at the broad background to what Silberman and several of our speakers have said about this alternative interpretation. In the late 13th and 12th centuries B.C.E., the entire east Mediterranean world was shaken to its core. Migrations and a massive social and economic breakdown brought on significant major changes, heralding the end of Late Bronze Age civilization and the dawn of the new Iron Age. The Hittite empire in Anatolia collapsed; the Egyptian empire drew to a close; the Mycenaean citadels of Greece fell into ruin; cities on the Levantine coast were destroyed. The great palace economies of the Late

Bronze Age had grown tired, too unwieldy and economically bankrupt to survive. The so-called Sea Peoples, spreading their own brand of destruction, moved by land and water from the Aegean into eastern states and empires already weakened by internal decay.

Out of this time of international troubles came a host of new political, social, and economic units: the Phoenician city-states of the Levantine coast, the Aramaean kingdoms of inland Syria, the late Hittite cities of northwest Syria, Philistine rule in coastal Palestine, and so on. The whole Mediterranean world had undergone a vast and permanent watershed of history—the crisis of the 12th century B.C.E.

The new model for the origin of the Israelites comes out of the maelstrom of the shift from the Late Bronze to the Iron Age. Native Canaanites moved into the Palestinian hill country and established a simple agrarian culture based on what they had known before but with its own unique features created to adapt to the demands of agriculture and social life in the mountains. The archaeological evidence is abundant—the hundreds of small villages and settlements in the hills. The early Israelites are now identified as the builders of these villages. This picture of the early Israelites is quite different from that of Joshua's warriors, who crossed the Jordan River and took the land by storm. But it is a far more realistic one. The archaeological record does not include Joshua's armies, but speaks rather in favor of a less exciting but verifiable alternative. Thundering battles and the trumpets at Jericho have given way to quiet village life and terrace farming.

The question one immediately asks, of course, is why the literary account should be so different from the reality presented by the facts in the ground. Why the thrilling exit from a land of bondage and the triumphant entry into a new land when there is nothing other than the biblical story itself that even hints at the thrill and the triumph? Were it not for that literary account, neither the Exodus nor the Conquest would be known at all. No one else paid any attention.

It has to do with the way history was recorded in antiquity and the biases of the ancient scholars who did the recording. It has been suggested that the literary account ultimately derives from folk memory, that is, the collective memory of a people, usually an oral tradition, handed down for generations. Now folk memories do not come into existence out of nothing. Folk memories, the oral tradition of a family, a tribe, or a people, arise out of *something*. There is a kernel of historic fact buried there somewhere. It may be totally obscured by later elaboration, additions, explanations, or whole episodes grafted on just because they make a good story; or, as has been proposed, a faint remembrance that at one time in the past a few of those who would later become Israelites were in Egypt and migrated to Canaan, and this was associated in later tradition with some other historical age, such as the Hyksos period. This is one of the hallmarks of ancient historical writing: the folk memories, with all their elaboration, have become real history and are ultimately written down as real history. One need only glance at history as recorded by Herodotus or Manetho to see this. Hebrew scholars who wrote and edited their own national history belonged to the same tradition. This was the way history was put together, and the same methodology was still in force with Josephus, Eusebius, and a host of others.

Then there is the bias of ancient historical writing. Whether we look at Egyptian royal annals, or Babylonian historical texts, or the Old Testament, we must understand the perspective from which any ancient scholar viewed the world in which he lived.

Some years ago I read a history of the American Revolution written by an Englishman. There were things in that book none of us ever learned in school. Character flaws of George Washington, for example, that an American author might choose to ignore but which an English writer can discuss freely because George Washington is not the father of *his* country. An American historian would tend not to emphasize George's foul language or his avid pursuit of village maidens. An

English historian revels in such information. To us, the colonists were noble freedom fighters; to an Englishman, they were rebels against a legitimate government. And they didn't fight fair, either, because they hid behind trees. In other words, it is a matter of perspective. We view the history of another culture without the sentiment with which we view our own. And in writing our own history, we record what is important to us, to our society, to our past, and to our children whom we want to appreciate that history.

The Exodus and Conquest were recorded by Hebrew scholars because these events were significant to them and to their children. These events, or whatever it was that originally inspired them, were ignored by the rest of the ancient world because to the rest of the ancient world they had no significance at all. This suggests that the actual events themselves—those little kernels of history embedded in there somewhere—were minor, since they have left no trace except in the record of the people to whom they happened. The historical kernel for the Exodus may have been only one family peacefully migrating from Egypt to Palestine. The historical kernel for the Conquest may have been nothing more than a few skirmishes as disenchanted Canaanites left the coastal regions to build their small agricultural settlements in the hill country. A family moving from Egypt to Canaan could well become the majestic saga of a whole people, complete with plagues, Pharaoh's army, and seas giving way. A few minor fights up in the hills could well become the heroic struggle of a whole people against overwhelming odds, complete with the burning cities, the vast destruction, a sun that stopped moving for a while, and walls that tumbled when the trumpets blew.

Heroes and heroic events often grow from the small things that happen, even when the small thing is unimportant and not the stuff of which sagas are made. It still happens that way. John Brown, a rather unsavory character, became a folk hero of the American Civil War. But the fight at Harper's Ferry was an insignificant event and Brown himself an insignificant individual who was hung as a traitor by the state of Virginia. Still, public reaction at the time helped ignite the whole country. So today we sing the legend of an unimportant man—his soul goes marching on—because of a minor deed that happened to spark the imagination of his contemporaries. And that is how folk history comes into being.

Now all this allows only a partial answer to why the Exodus-Conquest as told in the ancient literature is so different from the actual facts as they are now emerging. For the Conquest part of the equation, the archaeological situation seems clear enough, and I rather like the idea that a few skirmishes in the hill country provide the kernel of reality that gradually grew into the national epic of military conquest under Joshua. These proto-Israelites, after all, did create a new society in the region that would later become the kingdom of David and Solomon, even though that new society was one of simple agrarian settlements rather than large urban centers, farmers instead of warriors. The Conquest, therefore, has roots in a real social movement, with a substantial mass of archaeological material to back it up. It is no longer the sweeping destruction wrought by Joshua's troops, but the roots are known—the historical kernel is there. It is quite in keeping with the development and recording of a national history that humble origins should later assume a more glorious aspect as the established Israelite monarchy looked back to record its past. We ourselves have consistently tidied up the story of our own revolution to shave off the rough edges.

But the Exodus remains a mystery. All except the most ardent defenders of a divine dictation of the narrative agree that it could not have happened the way it is set down. But for this event, there is no archaeological context into which it can be placed, no hint from Egypt from whence such hints would have to come. We still even have a problem with when it happened. The panel has suggested anywhere from the 15th to 12th centuries B.C.E., or that it was a series of movements throughout that period, or that it didn't happen at all. All we can currently produce are minor parallels here and there that show that foreigners did wander into Egypt and wander out again, that a much toned-down version of the biblical narrative could have happened, that the possibility of some historical kernel is there. But there is not a single iota of proof. Basically, Egypt remains uninterested and silent on the matter, as it always has.

If one were to characterize briefly the general thrust of this conference, it is that the empirical evidence of archaeology and language does not remotely resemble the biblical narrative of the Exodus and Conquest. That narrative grew out of a national history of the Hebrews, written by Hebrew scholars, for a Hebrew audience. Whether it arose from mistaken folk memories or from the elaboration and mythologizing of minor events, that narrative contrasts markedly to the total absence of direct Egyptian evidence to support the Exodus story and the growing body of evidence suggesting that the Conquest did not take place. The biblical and nonbiblical sources simply tell two different tales.

But this does not mean we are confronted with having to choose which one is correct or with having to harmonize the two into some kind of coherent whole. This has been the main error of two centuries of modern biblical study. We must, rather, understand that a choice is unnecessary and that it is impossible to create a coherent whole, for we are dealing with two totally different kinds of source material.

One is a literary tradition recording history as it was seen by ancient historians. They did not fabricate a narrative. They believed that a sea was rolled back, that the sun stopped in the heavens one day, that cities fell before the trumpet's blast. This is the way history was written in those days; you recorded what you believed had happened, not necessarily what you could prove had happened. Guillaum of Nangis, in his 14th-century history of France, records that a plague had fallen over the land because a two-headed calf had been born in a country village. This was a fact not to be questioned; he believed it and wrote it down as such. National histories tend to do that sort of thing. Thus we must see history in the Old Testament narrative not as it happened but as it was perceived to have happened, from the perspective of those to whom it happened.

The other source, the archaeological and linguistic record, tells us something of what really happened or didn't happen. That archaeology refuses to validate in any way the biblical narrative should not be surprising. And it does, after all, present a valid alternative. Until fairly recently, with the possible exception of the Merneptah Stela, the Hebrews did not appear at all in the archives of nonbiblical history until the time of the Divided Monarchy, when kings of Judah and Israel were listed among the petty rulers who paid tribute to the Babylonian and Assyrian empires. We can now push that historical recognition back into the early Iron Age. The Hebrews of the magnified and mythologized literary source are now identified as a real culture in a real time in a real place. That this culture is in its reality far less noble than in its literary description is beside the point. At least it is real.

This conference is, therefore, not about choosing between a historical narrative or the archaeological record. Nor is it about trying somehow to bring two kinds of evidence into a harmony that gives us one account instead of two. This conference has, rather, been concerned with evaluating two kinds of evidence within their own parameters. The literary record is history as perceived by ancient ideas of what constitutes history. The archaeological record is history as perceived through the material remains. We need neither choose nor harmonize, simply recognize each kind of evidence for what it is and forget the dual burden of choice and harmony; choice is not necessary, and harmony is not possible.